Managing Project complexITy

using

The Project Management Trifecta: Project Management, Agile, and Lean Six Sigma

First Edition

The complexITy Series

Shere L.H. McClamb

First published: October 2025

Published by The bITa Group
Publishing@TheBitaGroup.com
Benson, North Carolina 27504

ISBN: 9798218835002

Preface

This book explores how to use the Project Management Body of Knowledge, the Agile framework, and the Six Sigma methodology to manage projects. Seasoned project managers will benefit from a refresher on the tools and techniques of project management. Aspiring and new project managers will fill their toolbox with tools and techniques that can be scaled up to manage projects efficiently. The project management skills in this book are a must for anyone who manages a project, whether that is your official title or not.

The chapters of this book cover the essential elements of successful project management. Charts and other visual tools and techniques are illustrated to ensure the highest levels of comprehension, especially for visual learners. This includes comprehensive explanations of tools and techniques in the phases of initiation, planning, execution, and monitoring, and then closing the project.

It then explores what Agile is, its tools and techniques, and the different flavors of Agile, so that the chosen framework aligns with how the team will work to complete the project. For example, many project managers choose popular frameworks like Scrum or use Kanban boards. But this book takes its steps further, introducing Agile Methodologies that are less popular but highly effective for project management, such as Feature-Driven Development, Extreme Programming (XP), and Dynamic Systems Development Method (DSDM).

Finally, Six Sigma is introduced through the Define, Measure, Analyze, Improve, and Control (DMAIC) phases to make the project lean by removing waste and variation in the project management process. The introduction of essential Lean Six Sigma tools, such as Pulling Tasks on a Kanban Board, Efficiently using Heijunka, and Monitoring your improvements with Control Charts. By infusing these three practices into the process, the project manager is better able to adapt to changing project requirements and complete projects faster.

The number of failed projects has improved over the years, but there is still room for improvement. These three Frameworks together will bring the new project manager up to speed on the basics and give them the edge they need via the project management trifecta. A trifecta in horse betting is when you choose the three horses that will win a race. In a 'boxed trifecta, the 1st, 2nd, and 3rd place winners that are selected can cross the finish line in any order. I argue that each of these frameworks is a winner in their own right, and they work together in many ways. The trifecta will definitely increase the likelihood of delivering a successful project by managing deadlines, people, and changing priorities successfully. The tools and techniques are agnostic and introduce the skills required to lead effectively, regardless of the project's size or complexity.

You will gain an understanding of the following concepts from this book:

- Core project management principles
- Proactive approaches to risk management
- Leading productive teams
- Agile Project Management, using Kanban Boards, and other project methodologies
- Agile Manifesto Principles and Values
- Using Six Sigma to pinpoint problems and implement project process improvements
- Building a comprehensive methodology that allows you to manage work processes to successful outcomes.

Table of Contents

List of Figures

List of Tables

About the Author

Shere L.H. McClamb grew up in North Carolina, where she currently resides. She has more than 25 years of experience in the Information Technology field and is presently the Senior IT Project Manager for Durham County, North Carolina. Shere has led IT projects as the Transformation Manager for the NC Department of Public Instruction, a Senior Business Intelligence Analyst for the NC Government Analytics Center, a project manager for the NC Department of Public Safety, the Webmaster for the University of Saint Augustine's, and taught IT courses for Johnston Community College.

Shere holds a Ph.D. in Information Technology from Capella University, a Master of Arts in Organizational Leadership from Gonzaga University in Spokane, Washington, a Bachelor of Science in Business Administration from Mount Olive University in Mount Olive, North Carolina (on the corner of pickle and vine), Associate of Applied Science (AAS) degree in Network Administration and Support from Johnston Community College in Smithfield, North Carolina.

Shere's professional certifications include Project Management Professional (PMP) and Agile Certified Practitioner (PMI-ACP) Certifications from the Project Management Institute (PMI), an ITIL Foundations Certification, and ASQ Certified Six Sigma Black Belt Certification.

CHAPTER ONE: THE PROJECT MANAGEMENT TRIFECTA

Introduction

In this chapter, you will:

Learn why choosing a project management framework, tailoring your effort with agile, and using Six Sigma as a constant groomer is an absolute success trifecta for delivering project management value.

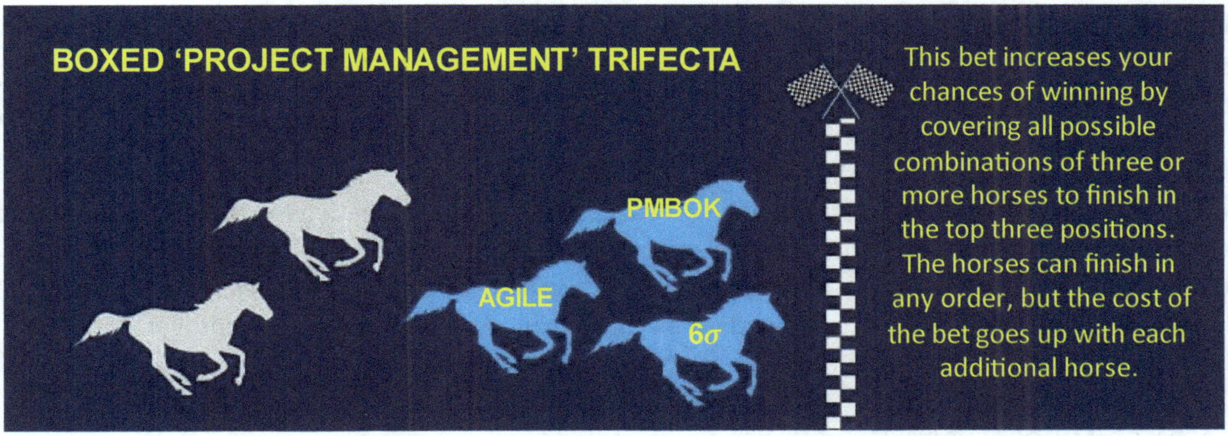

This book integrates the Project Management Body of Knowledge, Agile, and Lean Six Sigma to equip project managers with the tools to drive successful project outcomes. Combining the strengths of each of these ensures that the final product is within scope, of the best quality, delivered on time and within budget, and that the project process is infused with quality as well. This is, of course, what every project manager strives for, but realizing results is often complex and downright difficult. Many projects fail to achieve their goals not because of the strength or weakness of the project manager, but simply because they lack a well-rounded toolbox. As project and initiative managers, we must have all the tools in our toolbox to achieve successful outcomes.

The Project Management framework, an Agile mindset, and the Six Sigma methodology are introduced as the trifecta —and, to be sure, not in any particular order. Like horses in competitive races, there are many frameworks and methodologies in project management to achieve successful finishes. There are many ways to guide a project, and if it works for you, by all means keep on keeping on. The three introduced here are all winners in their own right and certainly do not need to lean on each other to be great. Instead, I pose that when these winners are brought together, they can take your projects from running smoothly to having awesome outcomes beyond just implementation.

Improving the discipline where the tools of project management, agile, and six sigma come together is a trifecta that benefits all project stakeholders. This book will lay the foundation for each of the three and show how the tools and techniques overlap and can be used together to achieve winning project outcomes. The overlap of project management, agile, and Six Sigma makes good sense. Let's start by looking at how the two foremost authorities on project management and process improvement describe their current landscapes. The authorities have offered the following:

PROJECT MANAGEMENT INSTITUTE (PMI)	ASQ	AGILE MANIFESTO
"the application of knowledge, skills, tools, and techniques to project activities to meet project requirements. It's the practice of planning, organizing, and executing the tasks needed to turn a brilliant idea into a tangible product, service, or deliverable".	"a method for disciplined quality improvement that provides the tools organizations need to improve the capability of their business processes".	"We are uncovering better ways of developing software by doing it and helping others do it".

Figure 1. The 3 Foundations of The Project Management Trifecta

Project Managers must constantly upgrade their education and skills to remain competitive and successful in this field. Adding discipline to projects is a valuable addition to traditional project management skills. Six Sigma will give you the statistical tools to move the project from ad hoc implementation and thinking, such as "I think" or "I believe", to "I'm absolutely sure". Six Sigma allows project managers to use Six Sigma to solve problems through empirical data by embedding statistically driven elements into their processes to move goals, requirements, processes, and decisions from vague to precise.

Even if you are running awesome projects, there are always areas that can be improved. For the rest of us, there are wastes (a six sigma term) such as schedule delays, rework that impacts the budget, and the frustration of quality misalignments that we can squeeze out of our projects.

The benefits of Agile methodologies have been well established for several years, and most projects currently use a hybrid approach. Agile and hybrid project management approaches are defined by the project manager and the project management team as the project dictates. The 12th principle of the Agile Manifesto states "at regular intervals, the team reflects on how to become more effective, then tunes and adjusts its behavior accordingly." Agile teams are focusing on continuous improvements, which fits hand-in-glove with the creed of Six Sigma." There is an entire chapter dedicated to Agile to familiarize you with agile methods you know and maybe some that are not as popular, which you may find helpful.

Six Sigma uses statistical methods to identify defects in the measurements. It aims for just 3.4 defects per million opportunities, which translates to 99.99966% accuracy in project delivery. Six Sigma within traditional projects infuses data and statistical analysis, enabling a better understanding of customer requirements — especially when they are unclear and ever-changing — and uncovering variations and deficiencies across all parts of the project process that can be improved.

Running a strong project starts with remembering the core message of Agile, which states, "Our highest priority is to satisfy the customer through early and continuous delivery of valuable software (https://agilemanifesto.org/principles.html). The next step is building a strong project team. A project manager who understands agile project and initiative management, and a black belt who manages the project's processes, are required to move the project toward successful completion.

For aspiring project managers, this book lays a solid foundation of tools and techniques required to manage a project successfully. It lays out the elements found in the project management body of knowledge.

Project Management: Moving through the project management phases of initiating, planning, executing, monitoring, and closing a project. The artifacts required for typical projects are introduced with detailed figures and tables to support a deeper understanding. Projects vary in scope, time, and budget, so it will be up to you to determine which artifacts are best suited to the project at hand.

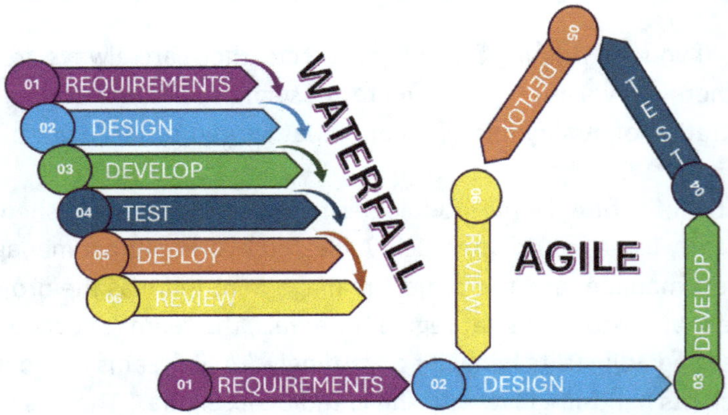

Some projects are documentation-heavy, requiring all the introduced artifacts, while others need only the artifacts that keep the project moving forward. This is where experience is needed. The project Sponsor and team will lean on you to provide what they need, when they need it, to be successful. Carefully learn all of the tools to manage a project and then thoughtfully choose what the project calls for. This can be tricky, and sometimes you won't be given clear direction. As a novice project manager, preparing initiation artifacts that will not be disseminated is a great way for you to wrap your arms around the entire project.

To have a strong foundational understanding of the who, what, when, where, and whys of the project so that you can speak to and answer any questions with the authority you have been given to lead the effort.

Agile: Most projects today are iterative in some way. Gone are the days when organizations spend up to a year gathering and consolidating requirements to kick off a project. Project managers are required to manage projects throughout the requirements-gathering process.

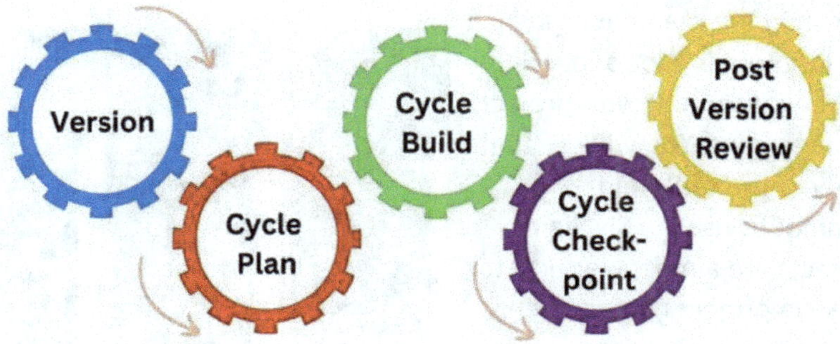

Many times, the product of the projects is a well-conceived concept, but how to get there is less clear. In these cases, the project manager is asked to manage the process of gathering the requirements needed to create or develop the project. This most always involves an evolutionary process of asking the right questions, designing from what was heard, developing a part of the product, and seeing if you got it right. If not, try again until it is right and then build upon the success. This iterative process is repeated until the product has fulfilled the initial vision. Agile requires discipline, cooperation, and constant communication, and as the leader of the endeavor, it is your job to keep all the pieces moving smoothly and in a forward direction. Planning iterations, grooming requirements, having meetings with the project team, and utilizing feedback are all part of the work of the agile project manager.

This book not only lays out the primary tools and techniques of Agile Project Management, but also explains the different flavors of agile you can use to build the project team you need to deliver the product. One of the great things about Agile is that it is not a one-size-fits-all approach to project management. Even though frameworks like SCRUM are very popular, others like Feature Driven Development (FDD), the Dynamic Systems Development Method (DSDM), and the Crystal Agile Framework may work better for the project. Learning the major agile frameworks and methodologies makes using Agile, even in a hybrid way, a strong choice.

Six Sigma: Six Sigma is all about statistical variation using the Define, Measure, Analyze, Improve, and Control method. If you are leading a project, believe me, you have some. Although Six Sigma is well known in the manufacturing world, there is a lot of overlap and enhancement with project management. You will see that many of the tools and techniques used in Six Sigma projects are almost identical to those in project management. As we strive to manage projects to the best of our ability, with the tools we have and within restraints, there is room for improvement. There is room for improvement in the project's product and in its management.

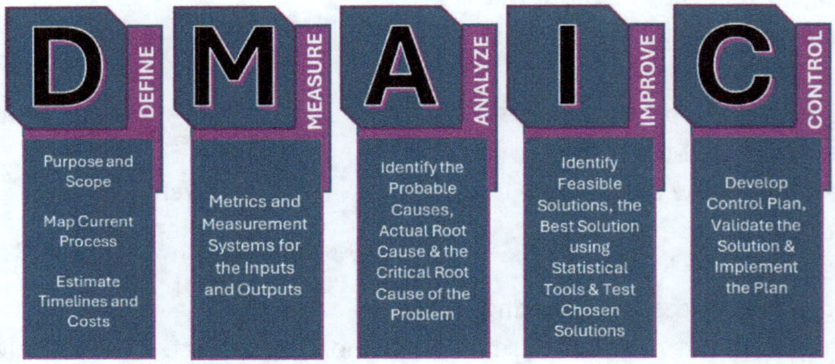

This is where Six Sigma shines! The whole point of Six Sigma is to review a process, identify problems, issues, or wastes, measure them, fix them, and finally make sure they stay fixed. Of course, this is Six Sigma in its simplest form, but you will learn how to do just that. Six sigma uses the phase to define the problem, issue, or waste, measure the occurrences to ensure you really have the problem you think you do, analyze how bad or how often it occurs, plan and implement Improvements, and finally control the improvements to make sure they stay fixed.

Using the Trifecta is the winning strategy for project managers.

CHAPTER TWO: THE PROJECT MANAGEMENT LIFE CYCLE

A walk through the essentials for the modern Project Manager

In this chapter, you will:

- learn the 5 phases of project management
- learn the artifacts that a PM should know how to create
- learn key tools and techniques

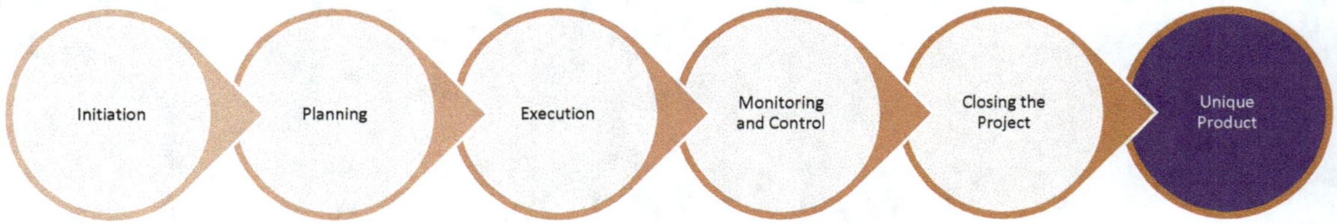

Figure 2. Project Management Phases

In this section, we will examine the phases, tools, and techniques of project management. In some form or fashion, we have all been project managers at one time or another. We often think of project management as applications or processes in the workplace. But the truth is, anytime you have created something unique from beginning to end, you have managed to project. A simple, long-standing definition of a project is: any endeavor that has a beginning and an end with a group of activities in the middle.

We will cover what is meant by a 'unique' product, determining the expectations or scope of a project, the team you will need to assemble to get the work done, creating and working on the activities that require undertaking, and last, but not least, keeping up with the funds dedicated to the effort.

There are five stages of project management. Initiating, planning, execution and monitoring, and closing the project. Moving through these stages will all make perfect sense by the end of this section.

The three major categories of a project are the product it produces, the people involved in its life, and the tools and processes they use to complete the work.

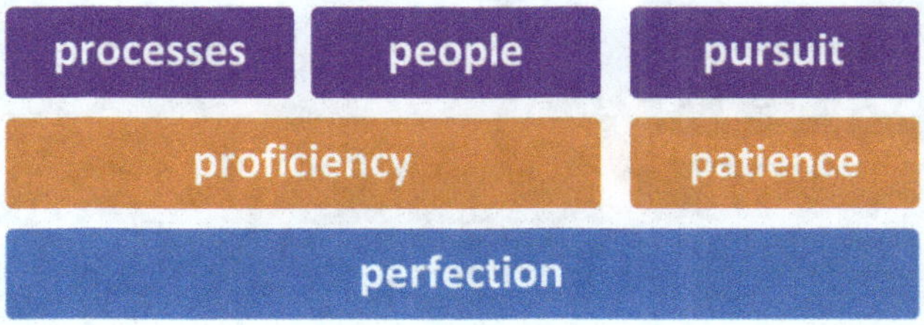

Figure 3. The 5 P's

Within this construct, the project manager seeks Ps: the processes used, the people involved, and the proficiency with which the project activities are executed. Some other awesome Ps are the passion with which the project is executed, the patience required to complete it, and the pursuit of perfection.

PROJECT MANAGEMENT PHASES

To successfully complete a project, you will meticulously move through the five phases of project management.

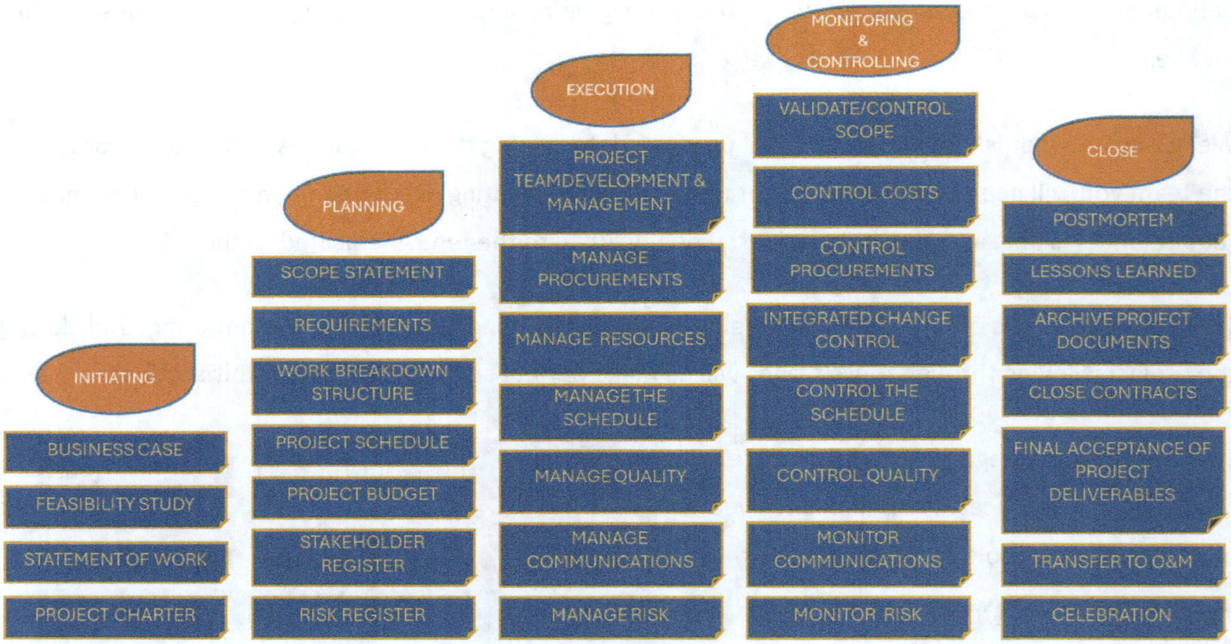

Figure 4. Project Management Phases

The first phase of a project is called Initiation. It is during this time that the idea becomes a concept, and the initiation, documentation, planning, and work follow. The second phase of a project is the planning phase. It is during this time that the project manager assesses all the elements needed to bring the project to fruition.

INITIATION

Figure 5. The Initiating Phase

I am moving pretty fast here, but I don't want to underemphasize the importance of planning in the conception and initiation phase of a project. When you decide to take a cruise, one of the first things that you will determine is what type of cruise you are interested in going on. There are many different types of cruises. There are river cruises, ocean cruises, singles cruises, family cruises, adults-only cruises, couples' cruises... You get the picture. The plans for each of these different types of cruises will be very different. Understandably, plan to book a singles-only cruise and end up on a family-only cruise with built-in babysitters and family-friendly activities. I can see how you might be very upset. Project definition is the same. It is imperative to define precisely what the project intends to produce. Determining the product that will be created, who will make it (or will you buy it), how much it will cost and how long the process will take is fleshed out when creating a business case, running a feasibility study, creating a statement of work and then creating the charter that pulls all of this information together to be signed by the sponsor that will guide the project.

The Business Case

When creating a business case in the initiation phase, it must include four elements to be successful. The creation of the business case is an endeavor undertaken by the person responsible for the product or service that the project will deliver. The goal of the business case is to determine whether the product or service is really needed, the best way to achieve the goal, and the cost in dollars and resources. The business case helps leaders determine whether the organization can deliver the product or service.

First is the problem and the business need. What needs or gaps have been discovered that require a project? In many cases, the business sponsor or someone in executive leadership will bring an idea for a product or software application to the project management office that makes things more efficient or effective. It is then that the project manager is asked to create a business case to request funding and resources to move forward.

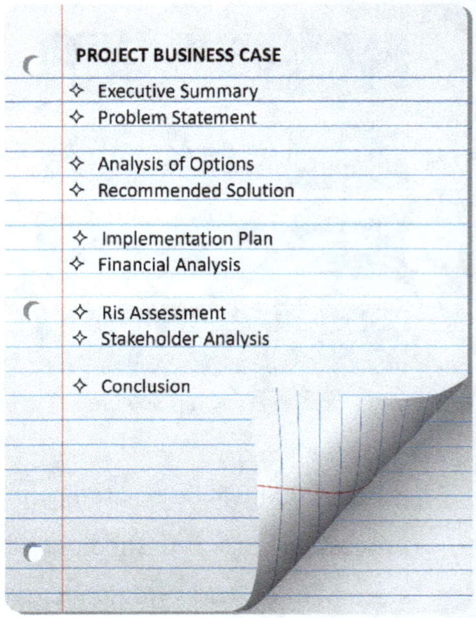

Figure 6. Project Business Case Sections

- The first section outlines the benefits and risks of undertaking the project.
- In the second section, you will outline the different solutions available to solve your problem, outlining alternative solutions.
- The third section is a financial section. It is here that the budget specifies the cost of the proposed solutions. And the return on investment.
- The last section of the business case is the final recommendation or preferred solution.

Key elements of a business case

Below are the sections of the business case that the leaders will use to weigh the pros and cons of the project.

Executive summary	A concise overview of the business case, highlighting the business problem, proposed solution, and expected benefits.
Problem statement	Describes the business issue or opportunity the project aims to address.
Analysis of options	An evaluation of the potential solutions, including their pros, cons, and estimated costs.
Recommended solution	The proposed course of action, along with a justification for its selection
Implementation plan	A high-level roadmap outlining the project timeline, milestones, necessary resources, and key deliverables.
Financial analysis	A cost-benefit analysis that breaks down the project's expected costs, benefits, and return on investment (ROI).
Risk assessment	The potential risks associated with the project and strategies to mitigate them, including sensitivity analysis.
Stakeholder analysis	A high-level view of the individuals or groups that the project impacts and their level of influence and interest.
Conclusion	The key points and offers a compelling call to action for decision-makers to approve the project.

Figure 7. Business Case Sections

The Feasibility Study

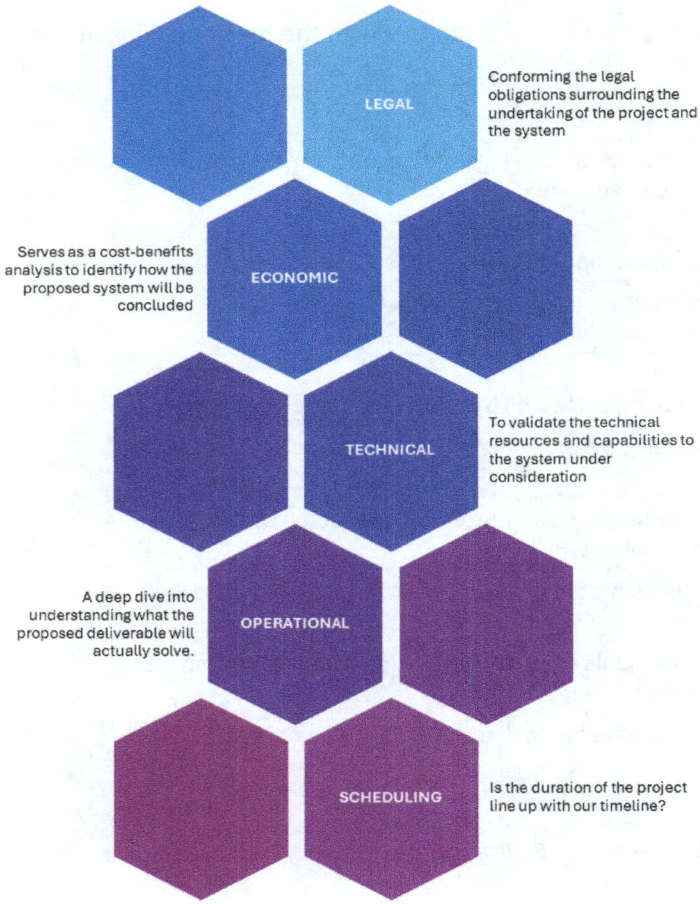

Figure 8. Types of Feasibility Studies

Feasibility studies help answer the essential question, "Should we proceed with the proposed idea?"

The five types of feasibility study are:

- Scheduling Feasibility
- Operational Feasibility
- Legal Feasibility
- Economic Feasibility and
- Technical Feasibility

The objective study may be completed in conjunction with a SWOT analysis, which assesses strengths, weaknesses, opportunities, and threats.

Feasibility studies help determine whether the company possesses the required resources or technologies, and whether the proposal offers a reasonable return vs. risk from the investment.

The most common feasibility study should include the following sections:

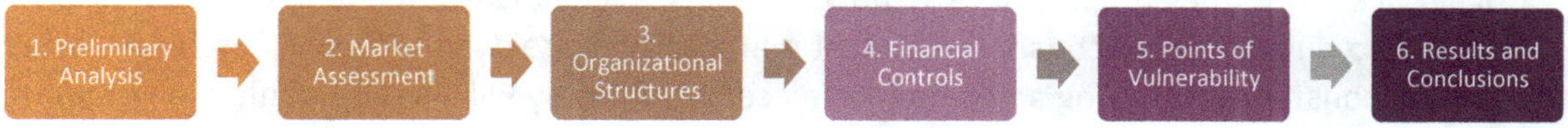

Figure 9. Common Feasibility Study Sections

- **Executive Summary:** provides an overview of the feasibility study document. Many people write this section after the rest of the document is completed. This section is essential because it allows for a high-level summary of the details in the rest of the document.

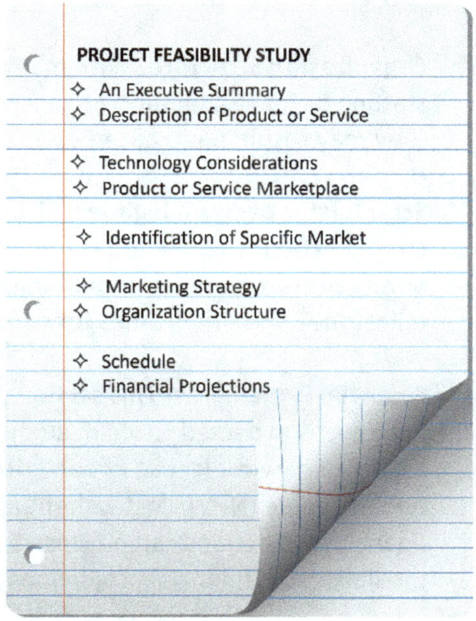

Figure 10. Feasibility Study Layout

- **Description of Product or Service** provides a high-level description of the products and/or services under consideration as part of the feasibility study. This section provides detailed descriptions of precisely what the organization is considering, so this information can be applied to the following sections of the document. This description must capture the most essential aspects of the products and/or services that the organization is considering, as well as how it may benefit customers and the organization.

- **Technology Considerations** outlines the technology-related considerations the organization must address. Many new initiatives rely on technology to manage or monitor various business functions. New technology may be developed internally or contracted through a service provider, and always results in costs that must be weighed in determining the path forward.

- **Product or Service Marketplace** describes the existing marketplace for the products and/or services the organization is considering. It may define who the target market consists of for these products or services, who the competitors are, how products will be distributed, and why customers might choose to buy our products/services. Most marketplaces are dynamic environments in which things change constantly. Entering a new marketplace unthinkingly will usually result in an organization not fully understanding its role and not fully maximizing its benefits.

- **Marketing Strategy** provides a high-level description of how the organization will market its product or service. Some topics that should be included are how the organization differentiates itself from competitors, the types of marketing it will utilize, and who it will target. Marketing efforts must be focused on the right target groups to yield the greatest return on investment.

- **Organization Structure:** With many new products or services, there may be a need for additional staffing or for restructuring to accommodate the change. These are important considerations as they may result in increased costs or require an organization to change its practices and processes.

- **Schedule:** provides a high-level framework for implementing the product or service under consideration. This section is not intended to include a detailed schedule, as one will be developed during project planning should this initiative be approved. This section may consist of targeted milestones and timeframes for completion, provided as a guideline only.

- **Financial Projections:** This section provides a description of the financial projections the new initiative is expected to yield, along with any additional costs. Financial projections are one key aspect of new project selection criteria. There are many ways to present these projections. Net present value (NPV), cost-benefit analyses, and balance sheets are just a few examples of how financial projections can be illustrated. This section should also provide the assumptions on which the illustrated financial projections are based.

The Statement of Work

A statement of work (SOW) is a document that describes the requirements of a given project.

It defines the scope of work, project deliverables, timelines, work location, and payment terms and conditions. Clarifies responsibilities and what's in and out of scope for your project.

This is crucial for aligning expectations and ensuring smooth project progress. Please share it with stakeholders to keep everyone on the same page throughout the project, prevent confusion, and improve collaboration.

- **Introduction:** Background that brought you to require the product under consideration; Objectives of the project; Reference to other applicable documents to support the project.

- **Staffing Roles and Responsibilities: Contractor Staff, Roles and Responsibilities** - Contractor staff involved; Individuals key to the project, detailed in a roles and responsibilities matrix; contractor tasks, staff, hours, rates, and cost. Include a function corresponding to the Org Chart. **Agency Staff, Roles and Responsibilities** - Who within the agency will have decision-making authority, including approval of changes, reports, documentation, and deliverables? Precise definition of all products, data services, and facilities the agency will provide; Include quantities, locations, and dates for delivery; Agency staff that will be involved; Individuals key to the project; Detail their roles and responsibilities.

- **Key Assumptions:** Identify/quantify: Any unknowns, Potential issues, any contractor and agency assumptions.

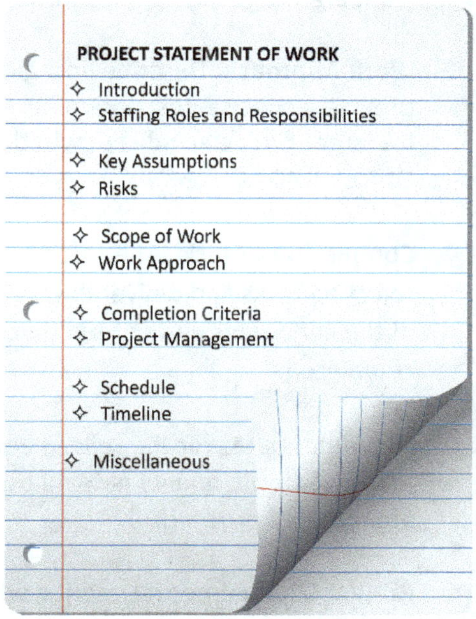

Figure 11. Project Statement of Work Layout

- **Risks:** Describe risks to the project and your proposed mitigation strategy. Require Contractor to identify any risks they are aware of and how they plan to mitigate the risks.

- **Scope of Work:**
  Inclusions- describe the tasks to be performed; resources assigned to tasks; costs associated with each task; location(s) where the task is to be performed; include functions that do not result in specific deliverables (i.e., project management); include tasks to be performed by the agency. Exclusions- Describe the functions that are not part of the scope of this project. **Deliverables:** Describe the items that will be developed or provided from the performance of the tasks (i.e. products, service, plans, status reports, documentation); Quantities, locations and dates for delivery; Periods of performance for services; Testing program plan; Implementation or migration plan to production; Are there Documentation Standards to be applied; If performance is a requirement, what are the reliability measures that will be used?

- **Work Approach:** Describe how the work is to be performed – if a formal methodology will be used, provide a concise description here. (E.g., "This project will use the PMBOK-based methodology. Also, for larger projects, indicate whether they will be tracked by the state CIO's Project Management Office (PMO).

- **Completion Criteria:** The focus of this section is to define the process for submitting, approving, and rejecting tasks and deliverables. **Final Acceptance Criteria:** Describe in detail the precise definition of the conditions and criteria that will be applied to determine that the contract has been completed.

- **Schedule:** Dates for the seller's key tasks or the completion of the project's significant elements. Identify interim quality gate milestones—decision points at which the project can be stopped or approved to proceed.

- **Project Management:** Describe what will be required as far as project management, which reports will be required, and what must be submitted to the state Project Management Office.

- **State Policies, Standards, and Computing Environment: Policies, Standards,** and Computing Environment. Double-check that the links point to the latest versions of the policies, standards, and environment.

- **Timeline and Period of Performance:** Outline the dates of the contractor's key tasks or submission of the product or service.

- **Compensation and Payment Schedule:** Compensation/Payment should be tied to completed tasks/deliverables approved by the agency. Require invoices to list the task ID, hours, deliverables, and the resource roles being billed for. List the details of compensation to be paid, e.g., hourly rates, number of hours per task, unit prices, cost per task, cost per deliverable, etc. Make it clear that the tasks and deliverables detailed in the invoice require the agency project manager's approval and sign-off before payment. Agency shall pay Contractor an amount not to exceed a certain amount that you will determine.

- **Miscellaneous:** Standards to be used, including hardware, software, and technical architecture, Travel and accommodations, Support personnel, Shipping, handling, and packaging, Conflict resolution agreement, Service level agreements, Performance standards, and other execution/signature blocks.

The SOW is the project contract that sets and aligns expectations. It summarizes the project's purpose and defines deliverables, standards, criteria, and requirements for each phase. The benefits of creating and using a Statement of Work are:

- Increased cost savings opportunities
- Supplier performance and risk mitigation
- Greater process efficiencies
- Detailed reporting
- Project performance management
- Visibility into all outsourced projects within a single purview
- Improved workforce management
- Organizational compliance and risk mitigation

The Project Charter

A charter helps head off misunderstandings down the road and puts the focus back on why the project was initiated in the first place. It is confirmation that everyone involved hears the same message. Once the project charter is developed and signed off by the project sponsor, it grants the project manager the authority to proceed with the project planning process and to apply organizational resources.

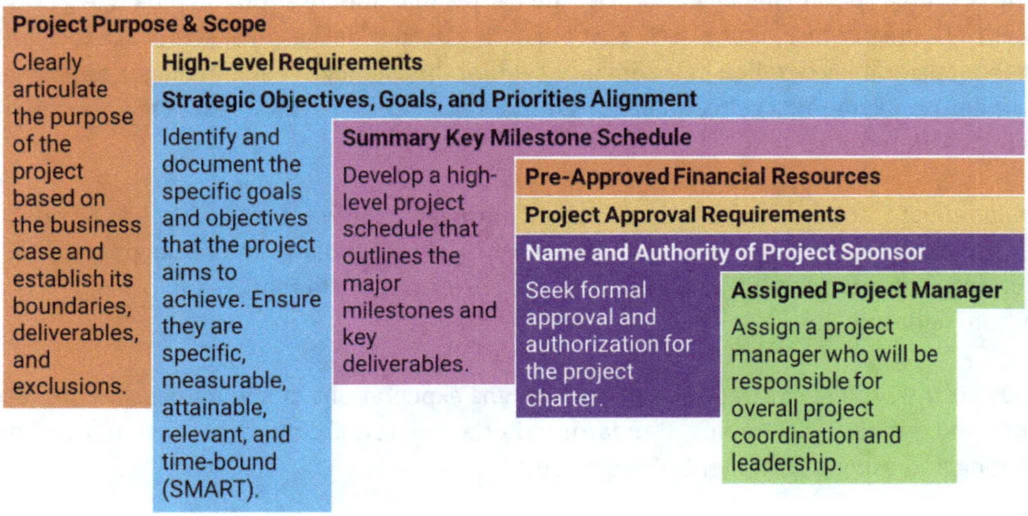

Figure 12. Project Charter Sections

WHEN TO USE IT: Create a charter every time you are placed on a project team. It serves as a starting point for planning and developing the project management plan. If you are on a project team in any capacity, ask to see the project charter! If one has not completed the project, one needs to create one.

WHO CREATES IT: The project charter is typically created by a combination of stakeholders, including the project initiator or sponsor, project manager, business analyst, and potentially some members of the project team. Input from these stakeholders helps ensure that the project charter accurately reflects the project's purpose, objectives, and scope.

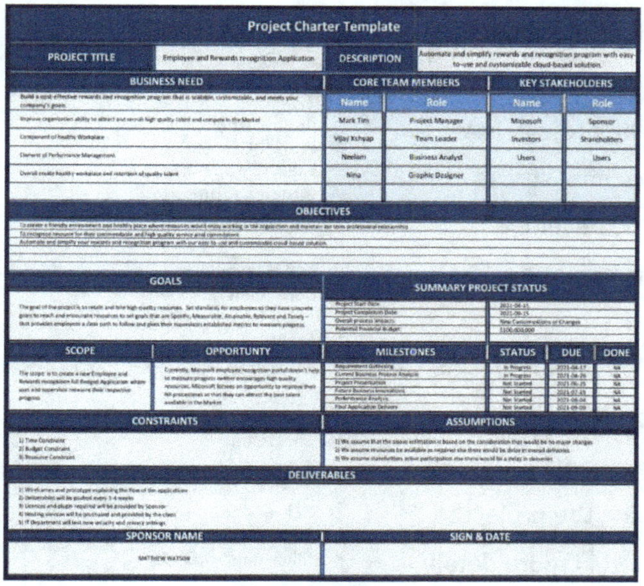

Figure 13. Project Charter Template Sample

WHO SIGNS IT: Creating a charter, whether it is written on a piece of paper, in an email that is shared, or a formal document that circulates for signatures, its importance should not be underestimated. By signing the project charter, the project sponsor formally authorizes the project to proceed and grants the project manager the authority to utilize organizational resources for the project's execution. It is not only for your protection, but also for the protection of your entire project.

GRASS ROOTS IT: Remember the purpose of the project charter. You need to know that you are working towards a thought-out initiative. Create one for yourself. Create a simple template from the items above and start to ask the questions to fill in the answers. Please place it in your named project folder. This is the start of many pieces of documentation you will create throughout the project.

The parts of the project charter include:

Project Title: Give your Project a title that is succinct and descriptive.

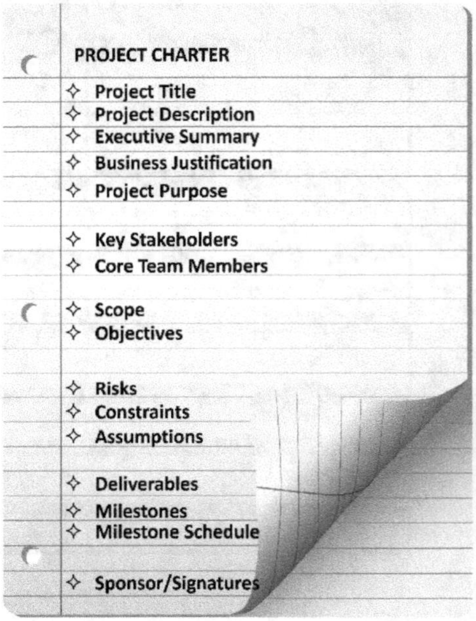

Figure 14. Project Charter Layout

- **Project Description:** a high-level description of the project. This description should not contain too much detail but should provide general information about the project, how it will be done, and what it is intended to accomplish. As the project moves forward, the details will be developed, but for the project charter, only high-level information should be provided.
- **Executive Summary:** a high-level summary of what issues or problems the project was created to correct. Typically, the executive summary also provides the background information and general statements regarding the project's purpose or justification, which will be covered in more detail in the appropriate section(s) of the charter.
- **Business Need:** the logic for the Business Need/Case (market demand, organizational need, customer request, technological advance, legal requirement, ecological impacts, social need, etc.). This section should also include the intended effects of the business case (i.e., cost savings, process improvement, new product development, etc.).
- **Core Team Members:** those who will participate as part of the project team throughout the project life cycle.

- ✧ **Key Stakeholders:** those with a significant interest in or who will be significantly affected by this project.
- ✧ **Objectives:** Describe the measurable outcomes of the project. Objectives should be SMART: Specific, Measurable, Attainable, Realistic, and Time-bound. The project manager must be able to track these objectives to determine whether the project is on the path to success. Vague, confusing, and unrealistic objectives make it difficult to measure progress and success.
- ✧ **Project Purpose / Business Justification** - the purpose and justification of the project in the form of a business case and objectives. The business case should explain the need for this project in terms of the business's function.
- ✧ **Scope:** List what the project will and will not address (e.g., this project addresses units that report into the Office of Executive Vice President. Units that report into the Provost's Office are omitted)
- ✧ **Risks:** Identify obstacles that may cause the project to fail. All projects have some form of risk attached. This section should list the high-level risks the project team has identified for this project.
- ✧ **Constraints:** List any conditions that may limit the project team's options with respect to resources, personnel, or schedule, as well as any restrictions or limitations the project manager must address regarding people, money, time, or equipment. It is the project manager's role to balance these constraints with available resources to ensure project success.
- ✧ **External Dependencies:** Will project success depend on the coordination of efforts between the project team and one or more other individuals or groups? Has everyone involved agreed to this interaction?

- **Assumptions:** identify the assumptions they will be working under as the project goes forward. These assumptions are what the project manager/team expects to have or be made available, without anyone specifically stating so
- **Deliverables:** list all of the deliverables that the customer, project sponsor, or stakeholders require upon the successful completion of the project. Every effort must be made to ensure this list includes all deliverables, and project sponsor approval must be obtained before adding any additional deliverables to avoid scope creep.
- **Milestones and Milestone Schedule:** Propose start and end dates for Project Phases (e.g., Inception, Planning, Construction, Delivery) and other major milestones. An estimated schedule of all high-level project milestones. It is understood that this is an estimate and will change as the project moves forward and the tasks, milestones, and their associated requirements become more clearly defined.
- **Sponsor/Signatures:** Name the individual who is ultimately responsible for funding and signing off on the project. Signature of all other key stakeholders (e.g., Project Manager)

The following are the benefits of a project charter:

- It gives the project manager the authority to complete the project.
- It explains the project's existence.
- It shows management's support for the project.
- It defines the outcome.
- It aligns the project with the organization's objectives.
- It gives team members a transparent reporting system.
- It helps avoid scope creep and gold plating.
- It helps prevent project disputes.

PLANNING

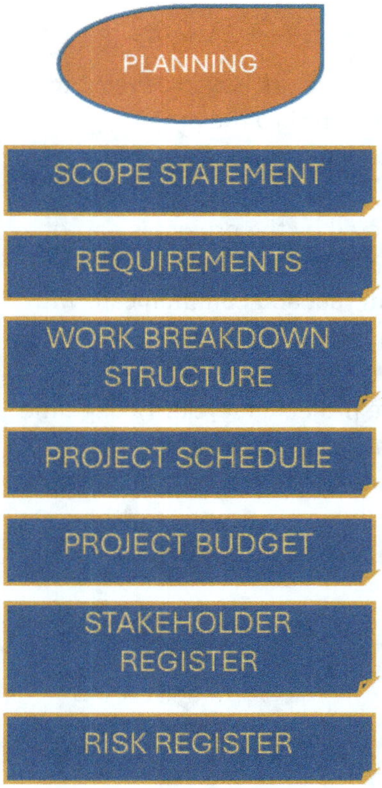

Figure 15. Project Planning Phase

Project managers spend a lot of their time planning their project's path forward. Good Project managers spend the time and effort setting their project up for success by focusing on the needs of the work. The scope statement is used throughout this process to guide the work.

In the planning phase, you and the project team will expound on the initial requirements collected in the initiation stage to complete the picture of what you will eventually deliver.

Project Requirements: We dive into what work needs to be completed, and the requirements often need revisiting. It is during the planning phase that requirements are fully fleshed out, enabling the creation of a work breakdown structure.

Work Breakdown Structure: A work breakdown structure (WBS) is a hierarchical, deliverable-oriented decomposition of a project. The work breakdown structure is an essential step in the planning process and should not be skipped. It is a helpful diagram for project managers because it allows them to break down their project scope and visualize all the tasks required to complete their projects.

Creating a WBS is the first step in developing a project schedule. It defines all the work that needs to be completed (and in what order) to achieve the project goals and objectives. By specifying the requirements, they will be decomposed into work packages. Using list and hierarchical formats, the work will be laid out into smaller units, usually at the task and activity levels. Not only is it used to create the project schedule, but it is also used when developing the budget and risk management.

Project Schedule: The project schedule is the backbone of the execution stage and should be carefully crafted. This task is made much easier by migrating the work breakdown structure into a spreadsheet or application where the work will be tracked as it's completed. Tools and techniques are used during this time to support planning and forecasting (e.g., schedule network analysis, three-point estimating, and precedence diagramming).

Project Budget: How much your project will cost and how you will pay for the work is also developed using the work breakdown structure and by adding key points or cost milestones to the project schedule. A milestone chart for costs is often used to outline project costs and the value created.

Project Stakeholders: Developing a registry of those who are on and affected by the project is part of the 'people' part of managing the project. Stakeholders, both inside and outside the project, will be explored. Moving from just a registry of names to insights as to how to interact and communicate with them to cultivate the best relationships based on trust and transparency.

Project Risk: Identifying and tracking project risk is an essential task in the project lifecycle. Taking time in the planning stage to actively identify and document all potential threats and opportunities that could impact a project's success —including listing all possible risks that might affect the project's deliverables, timelines, or budget during execution — is an absolute must. This also includes monitoring for the occurrence of a risk event, reassessing the risk (likelihood and consequences), monitoring the performance of the risk response plan, and reporting the results.

The Project Scope

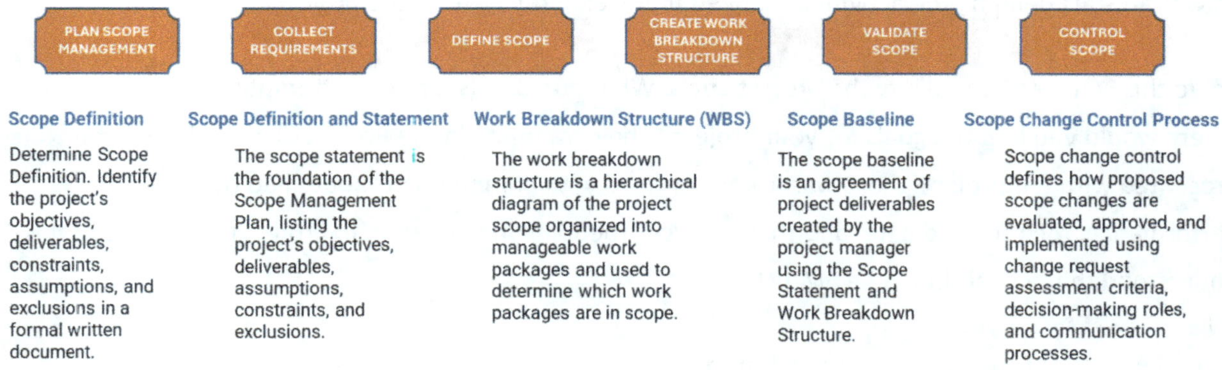

Figure 16. The Project Scope Phases

What do you want from us? That is the key question that the scope answers. What work does the project team need to complete to consider the project complete? It all starts here. In this section, we will explore the parts of the project scope and why it is important to define them when initiating your project. Determining what is in your project and what work will not be done is an essential part of a project manager's job. The project's aims should be written unambiguously.

The Scope Statement: The scope statement is meant to build a fence around what can be completed within the time and within the budget, and the quality of the project requires.

Project Goals and Objectives: Determining what's in and what's out of the project is the primary purpose of defining the scope. Defining the finished product is key.

A description of the results of the project should be clearly stated. There may be occasions when the ask exceeds what can actually be accomplished. When this happens, it is vital to make clear the items that will not be included in the final product. Remembering that a project creates a unique product. So, we will review our project Charter to look at the asks. Then we will create a Cascade into the objectives so we can start defining the activities we need to develop throughout the project.

To do this, you need to solidify the project goals. What outcome(s) are you attempting to achieve? So, where would you find the goals for your project? They are found in the Project Charter. When you were presented with the project, there was a want or need with parameters that defined the expected performance, the required date, and the resources (people, budget, etc.). In project management, it is understood that a goal should be SMART.

Figure 17. The SMART Definition

A good way to ensure a product is created to expectations and head off any misunderstandings is to define the acceptance criteria (AC) for the project's deliverables. Acceptance criteria are the conditions or boundaries a product must meet to confirm it is working as intended.

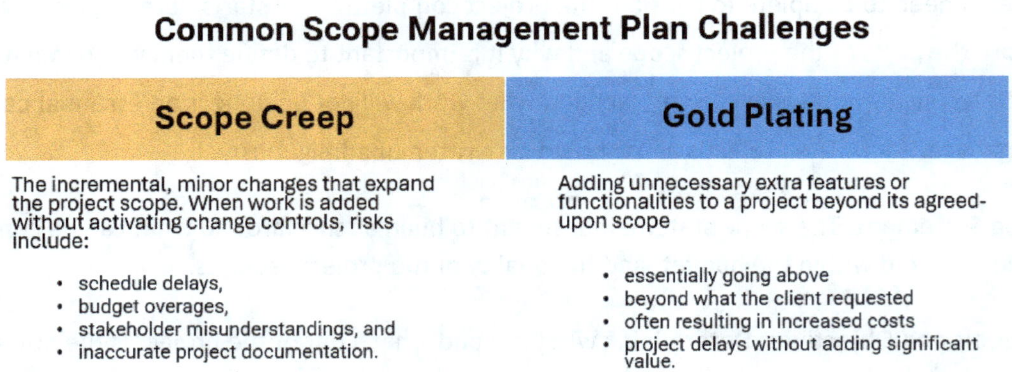

Figure 18. Scope Management Challenges

Other reasons for developing a well-thought-out project scope include minimizing the need to add work or features to a project once it's underway. Scope Creep is a term in project management that describes unauthorized work undertaken during a project. Incorporating work that is not listed in the project scope is a no-no. Adding work to a project's scope may increase the budget, schedule, or required resources. You can be on the lookout for signs of scope creep by ensuring that the statement of work is well thought through, the requirements are thorough, and you have not overpromised.

Promising or adding additional goodies to the work outlined is not considered scope creep because, technically, you have not expanded the work footprint; you have just given them gold when silver was scoped. This is called gold plating, and it is frowned upon as well. Even when it seems like a great idea to make the product even better than described in the scope, you will inevitably expend time or resources to make it happen.

The scope, schedule, budget, and quality of the product a project creates are often called the Iron Triangle. The reason the triangle analogy works is that if any side of the triangle is shortened, it causes the other sides of the triangle to correspond accordingly.

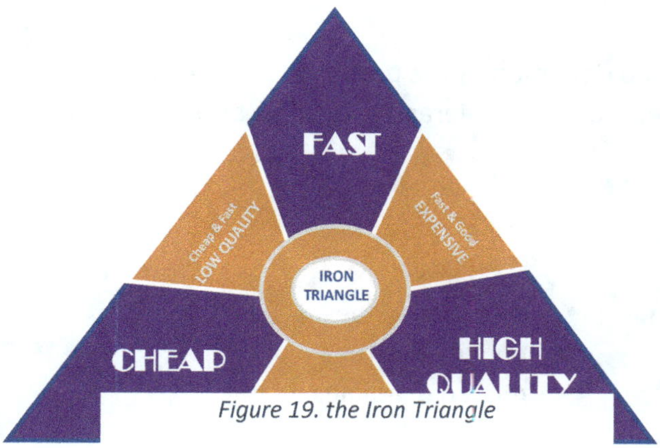

Figure 19. the Iron Triangle

Using the iron triangle as a premise, if you want the product to be cheap and fast, don't expect it to be high quality. If you are looking for a high-quality project, use a healthy budget and take the time needed to make it right. The third choice is not having the required funds and wanting a high-quality project; in most cases, the scope will have to decrease.

When changes to the scope of work are needed, the project must undergo formal change management to include them. Creating a plan to manage change is an essential part of scoping a project. Often, an idea leads to another, and it makes sense to include the work in the project. It needs to be clear how new work will be brought into the project and who will make those final decisions.

The Work Breakdown Structure (WBS)

The WBS is used as a starting point for scope management and is integral to other PMI processes, and, as a result, the standards that define these processes explicitly or implicitly rely on the WBS. It organizes and defines the project's scope and all work.

The Project Management Institute (PMI) Project Management Book of Knowledge (PMBOK) defines the Work Breakdown Structure as "a deliverable-oriented hierarchical decomposition of the work to be executed by the project team to accomplish the project objectives and create the required deliverables. Although PMI describes the WBS as hierarchical, it can be represented in various ways, including graphical, textual, and tabular views. Two common methods are the hierarchy diagram and the outline or tabular views.

Each descending level represents an increasingly detailed definition of the project work. The WBS is decomposed into work packages. The deliverable orientation of the hierarchy includes both internal and external deliverables." PMBOK® Guide

The benefits of a work breakdown structure include:

- scope creep
- unclear work assignments
- re-plans and extensions
- changing scope
- budget overruns
- missed deadlines

It represents an explicit description of the project's scope, deliverables, and outcomes—the "what" of the project. There are two types of WBS: 1) Deliverable-Based and 2) Phase-Based. The most common and preferred approach is the Deliverable-Based approach. The main difference between the two approaches is the Elements identified in the first Level of the WBS.

Deliverable-Based Work Breakdown Structure

A Deliverable-Based Work Breakdown Structure clearly demonstrates the relationship between the project deliverables and the scope. The definition of a deliverable according to PMBOK: Deliverable. Any unique and verifiable product, result, or capability to perform a service that must be produced to complete a process, phase, or project, and is often used more narrowly in reference to an external deliverable, which is a deliverable that is subject to approval by the project sponsor or customer.

Not to reinvent the wheel, this graphic from the Essentials of Project Management gives a great example:

Phase-Based Work Breakdown Structure

Level 1 elements are the phases of a project, and level 2 elements are the unique deliverables in each phase. All lower-level elements are deliverables. The work you have to accomplish throughout the project lifecycle is a great example of a phase-based work breakdown.

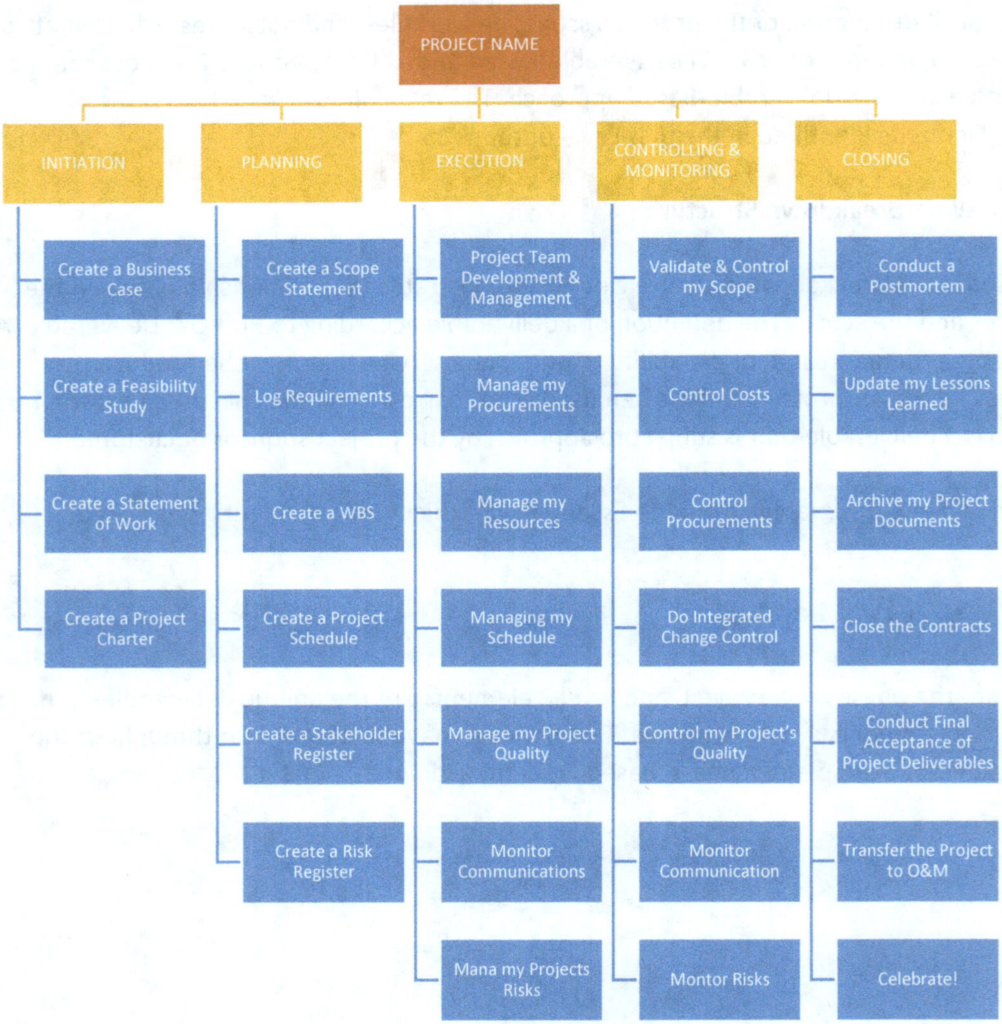

Figure 20. Sample Work Breakdown Structure of a Project

Creating a Work Breakdown Structure

A good Work Breakdown Structure is created iteratively by following these steps.

- ☐ Gather critical project documents.
- ☐ Identify content containing project deliverables, such as the Project Charter, Scope Statement, and Project Management Plan (PMP) subsidiary plans.

- ☐ Identify the appropriate project team members.
- ☐ Analyze the documents and identify the deliverables.

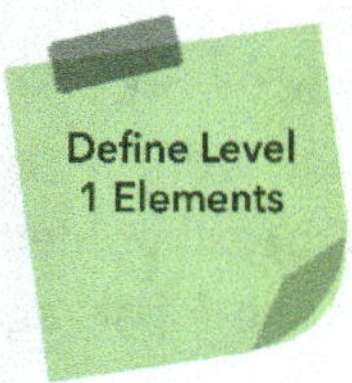

- ☐ Define the Level 1 Elements. Level 1 Elements are summary deliverable descriptions that must capture 100% of the project scope.
- ☐ Verify 100% of the scope is captured. This requirement is commonly referred to as the 100% Rule.

    - **Explanation of the 100% rule in more detail:** The 100% Rule (Haugan, 2002, p. 17) is one of the most important principles guiding the development, decomposition, and evaluation of the WBS. This rule states that the WBS includes 100% of the work defined by the project scope and, by doing so, captures all of the deliverables—internal, external, and interim—in terms of work to be completed, including project management. The rule applies at all levels within the hierarchy: the sum of the work at the "child" level must equal 100% of the work represented by the "parent," and the WBS should not include any work that falls outside the actual scope of the project; that is, it cannot include more than 100% of the work. *[Brotherton, S. A., Fried, R. T., & Norman, E. S. (2008). Applying the work breakdown structure to the* *project management lifecycle. Paper presented at PMI® Global Congress 2008—North America, Denver, CO. Newtown Square, PA: Project Management Institute.]*

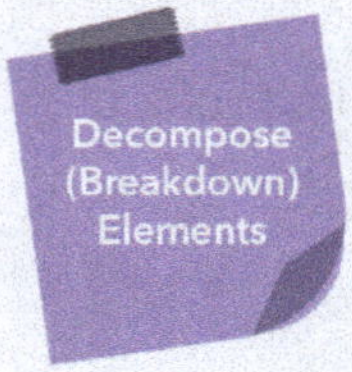

First, it is important to have a good definition of decomposition. Decomposition is "a planning technique that subdivides the project scope and project deliverables into smaller, more manageable components, until the project work associated with accomplishing the project scope and deliverables is defined in sufficient detail to support executing, monitoring, and controlling the work" *(PMI, 2004).*

- ☐ Begin breaking the Level 1 deliverables into unique lower-level deliverables. This "breaking down" technique is called Decomposition.
- ☐ Continue breaking down the work until a single individual or organization covers each Element. Ensure that all Elements are mutually exclusive.
    - Definition of a work package. A deliverable or project work component at the lowest level of each branch of the work breakdown structure. The work package includes the scheduled activities and milestones required to complete the work package deliverable or project work component (PMBOK).
- ☐ Ask the question: Would any additional decomposition make the project more manageable? If the answer is "no", the WBS is done.

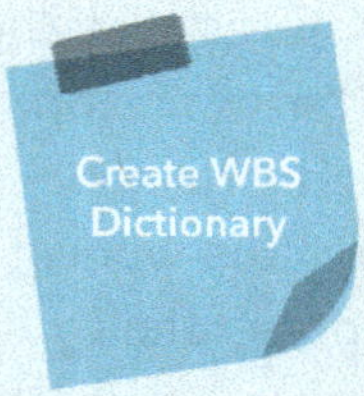

- ☐ Define the content of the WBS Dictionary. The WBS Dictionary is a narrative description of the work covered in each Element in the WBS. The lowest-level elements in the WBS are called Work Packages.
- ☐ Create the WBS Dictionary descriptions at the Work Package Level with enough detail to ensure that 100% of the project scope is covered. The descriptions should include information such as boundaries, milestones, risks, owner, costs, etc.

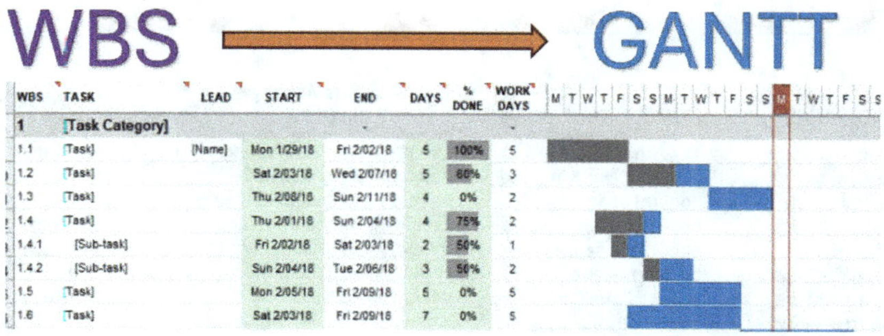

WBS	TASK	LEAD	START	END	DAYS	% DONE	WORK DAYS
1	[Task Category]			-			-
1.1	[Task]	[Name]	Mon 1/29/18	Fri 2/02/18	5	100%	5
1.2	[Task]		Sat 2/03/18	Wed 2/07/18	5	60%	3
1.3	[Task]		Thu 2/08/18	Sun 2/11/18	4	0%	2
1.4	[Task]		Thu 2/01/18	Sun 2/04/18	4	75%	2
1.4.1	[Sub-task]		Fri 2/02/18	Sat 2/03/18	2	50%	1
1.4.2	[Sub-task]		Sun 2/04/18	Tue 2/06/18	3	50%	2
1.5	[Task]		Mon 2/05/18	Fri 2/09/18	5	0%	5
1.6	[Task]		Sat 2/03/18	Fri 2/09/18	7	0%	5

- ☐ Decompose the Work Packages into activities as appropriate.
- ☐ Export or enter the Work Breakdown Structure into a Gantt chart for further scheduling and project tracking.

The Project Schedule

The schedule guides the project by defining how long all the activities that make up the project should take from start to finish. In the previous section, we reviewed the importance of and how to create a work breakdown structure. I hope you worked through that section diligently, because you won't be able to produce a good project schedule without it. If you skip the work breakdown structure work in your projects, it is not the end of the world.

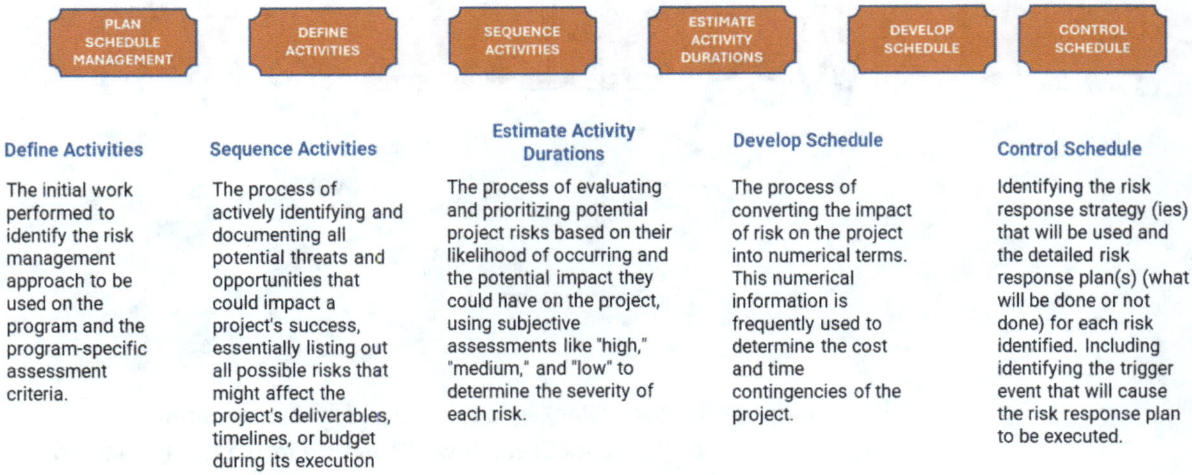

Figure 21. Project Schedule Phases

Many project managers combine the WBS and create a single schedule that covers the work required to create the WBS.

There are seven distinct steps when creating the project schedule.

Table 1. Project Schedule Creation Steps

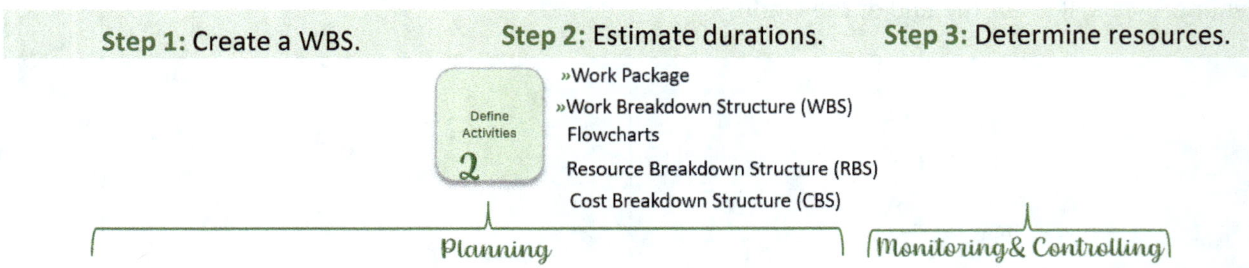

Step 4: Identify predecessors.

Dependency Determination

- Factors that may significantly affect the ranking of activities. That's why dependencie s need to be determined to sort out activities.

Leads and Lags

- Lag can be defined as the total amount of time when a successor activity is delayed after the predecessor activity.
- A Lead is exactly the reverse of a lag. In network diagrams, it is an acceleration in a successor activity.

Precedence Diagramming Method (PDM)

- Data representation that visually reveals the logical relationships between activities and activities, the priority relationship.

Step 5: Identify Dependencies

Organizational Process Assets

- Project dependencies mentioned in the portfolio and program plans, existing planning procedures, templates, and lessons learned repository are useful inputs.

Enterprise Environmental Factors

- Existing standards of the industry, Project management information system, scheduling software in the market are examples of EEF to use.

Step 5: Determine Milestones

Milestones are indicators of the project's progress, significant moments in the project, or points at which contract expenditures are paid to vendors for work accomplished. When placing milestones on your schedule, remember that milestones do not have durations; they are simply stopping points for actions within the project.

Milestones are often a signal from one phase to the next. At this time, the project team will be asked to review a batch of work. Some project managers use milestones as starting points when creating project schedules, while others use them once the schedule is made to break the project into manageable chunks of work.

A project roadmap is often composed solely of project milestones to provide a high-level view of the project. There are many vibrant templates you can use when creating a milestone roadmap.

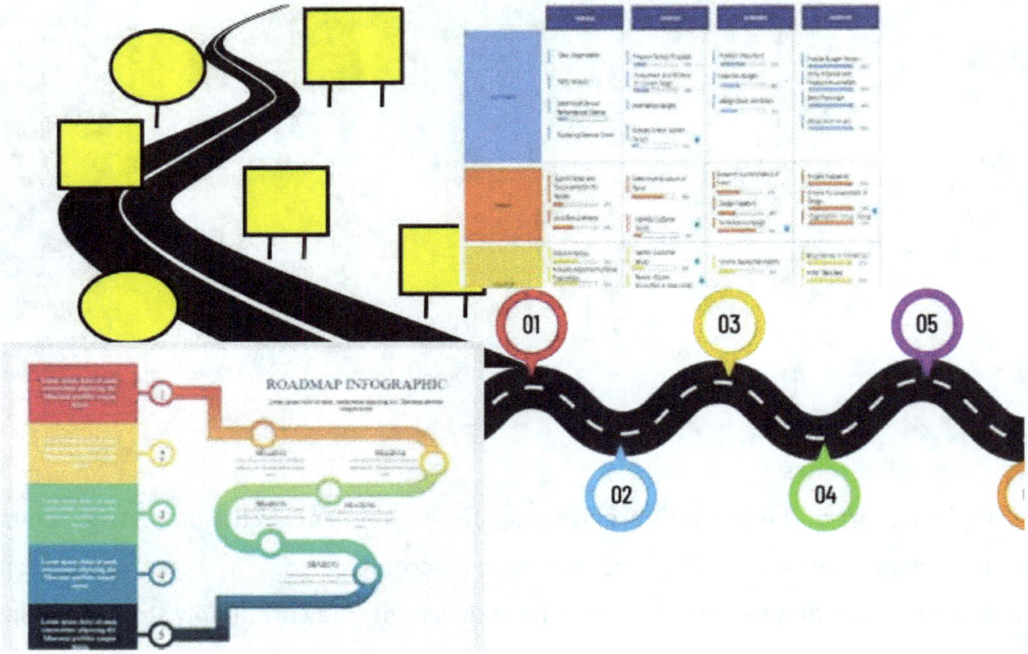

Figure 22. Determining Milestones

Step 6: Develop Schedule

Add:

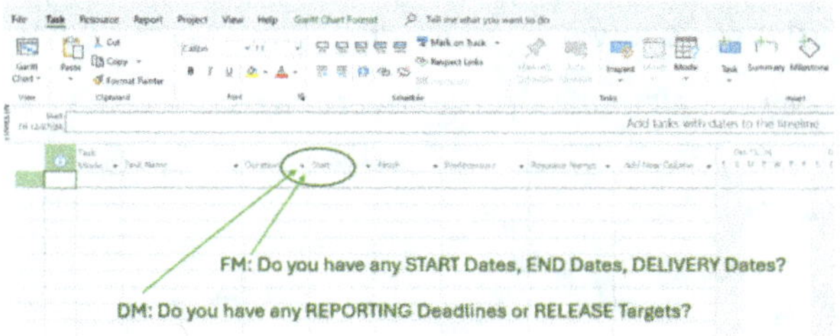

- Fixed Milestones (FM)
- Discretionary Milestones (DM)

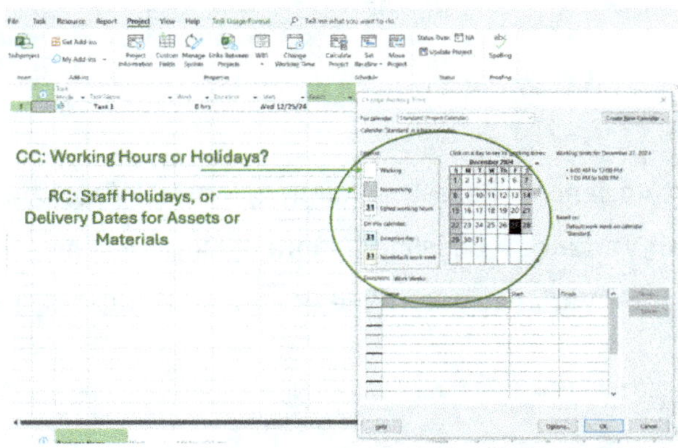

- Calendar Constraints
- Resource Constraints
- Working Hours

Then Add:

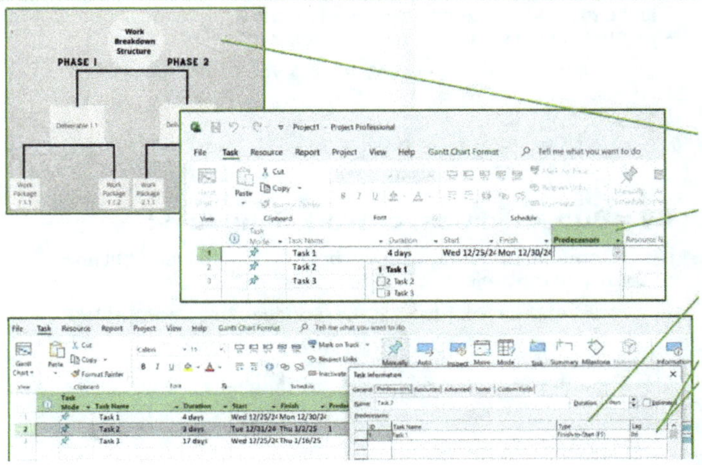

- Tasks
- Predecessors
- Dependencies (F to S)
- Lags
- Leads

Step 7: Control Schedule – Schedule Variances

Schedule Variances show how much the project is ahead or behind schedule. Baselining the project schedule is key to calculating project variances.

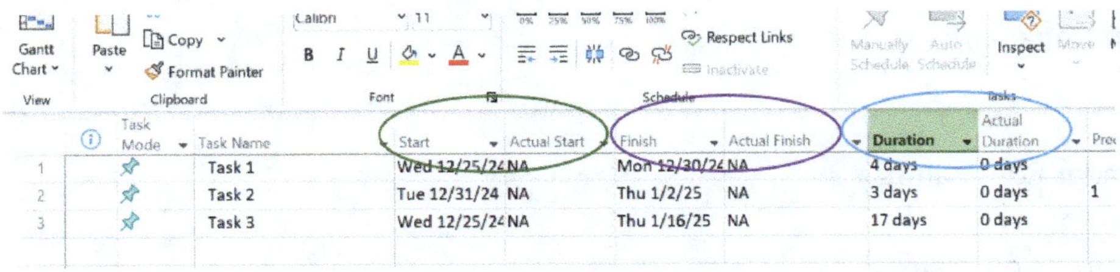

Task Start Variance = Baseline (Planned) Start – When the Task Actually Started

Task Finish Variance = Baseline (Planned) Finish – When the Task Actually Finished

Task Duration Variance = Baseline (Planned) Duration – How long did it actually take to finish the Task

This can be confusing because even though you are calculating the schedule you will be using the budget

EV = Budgeted Cost of Work Performed

It is the money we should have spent for the work we have completed – we are going to value it using our *planned cost*

Actual Percentage of the work you have completed

x

How much work you Planned for the work to Cost

Earned Value (EV) = Actual % Complete x Total Budget

Planned Value (PV) = Planned % Complete x Total Budget

PV = Budgeted Cost of Work Scheduled

It is the amount of work we should have accomplished until now according to the project schedule

Planned Percentage of the work you have completed

x

How much you Planned for the work you have completed to Cost

Schedule Variance (SV) = Earned /value – Planned Value
Schedule % = Schedule Variance (SV)/Planned Value
Schedule Performance Index (SPI) = Earned Value/Planned Value
To Complete Schedule Indicator (TSPI) = Total Budget – EV)/(Total Budget-PV)

>1 = Ahead of Schedule

Good: You did *more* work than was scheduled

| <1 = Ahead of Schedule

Not so Good: You did *less* work than was scheduled

Term	Formula
Earned Value	EV = PV to date × RP
Cost Variance	CV = EV – AC
Schedule Variance	SV = EV – PV
Cost Performance Index	CPI = EV/AC
Schedule Performance Index	SPI = EV/PV
Estimate at completion	EAC=BAC/CPI
Estimated time to complete	Original Time Estimate/SPI

The Project Costs and Budget

Project cost management is primarily concerned with the cost of resources needed to complete the tasks and activities in the project schedule. When determining the costs, the project manager should also consider the effect of the project decision on the cost of using, maintaining, and supporting the product, service, or result of the project. When determining costs, we must remember that the project's stakeholders will measure costs differently at different times.

Estimate Costs	Determine the Budget	Control the Costs
The process of developing an approximation of the monetary resources needed to complete project activities. Includes identifying and considering various costing alternatives. The estimating costs process considers whether the expected savings can offset the cost of the additional design work.	The initial work performed to identify the risk management approach to be used on the program and the program-specific assessment criteria.	The initial work performed to identify the risk management approach to be used on the program and the program-specific assessment criteria.

Figure 23. Project Costs and Budgeting Phases

When estimating project costs, a quantitative assessment of the probable costs of all resources to complete the project is conducted. The first is the calculation of variable costs as production changes (wages); the second is the calculation of fixed expenses (Rental of the Building); and the last are direct costs (attributable to the project, travel) and indirect costs (overhead – administrative work).

> **Estimate Costs** is the process of developing an approximation of the monetary resources needed to complete project activities.

The Cost Management Plan is a component of the project management plan and describes how the project costs will be planned, structured, and controlled. It is important that you base the determinations on:

Includes identifying and considering various **costing alternatives.**

Units of Measure: Each unit used in measurements (such as staff hours, staff days, weeks for time measures; or meters, liters, tons, kilometers, or cubic yards for quantity measures; or lump sum in currency form) is defined for each of the resources

Level of Precision: The degree to which activity cost estimates will be rounded up or down based on the scope of the activities and magnitude of the project.

The **estimating costs process** considers whether the expected savings can offset the cost of the additional design work.

Level of Accuracy: The acceptable range (e.g., + ± 10%) used in determining realistic activity cost estimates is specified and may include an amount for contingencies.

For example, the organizational procedures linked from the WBS provide the framework for the cost management plan, ensuring consistency with budget estimates and cost control. The WBS component used for the project cost accounting is called the control account. Control Thresholds are important because they are used to monitor cost performance and may be specified to indicate the agreed-upon amount of variation allowed before some action is required.

For example, **additional work** during a design phase may have the potential for reducing the cost of the execution phase and product operations.

Analogous Estimating uses historical information and expert judgment. Values of parameters (scope, cost, budget, duration, size, weight, complexity) using actual costs of previous projects – "gross value estimating approach" that can be adjusted based on project complexity. Frequently used when time is limited, or little information is known about the project details. Less costly and time-consuming, but generally less accurate for new 'type' projects, MOST RELIABLE on projects that are recurring and like past projects (i.e., housing and construction industry).

Would you go on a cruise if you didn't know how much it was going to cost you?

Or what was included and what you would have to pay out of pocket for. Of course you wouldn't. Nor would you start a project without knowing how much the project would cost to complete. Breaking down these project elements and assigning costs to each is the work that goes into the cost management plan.

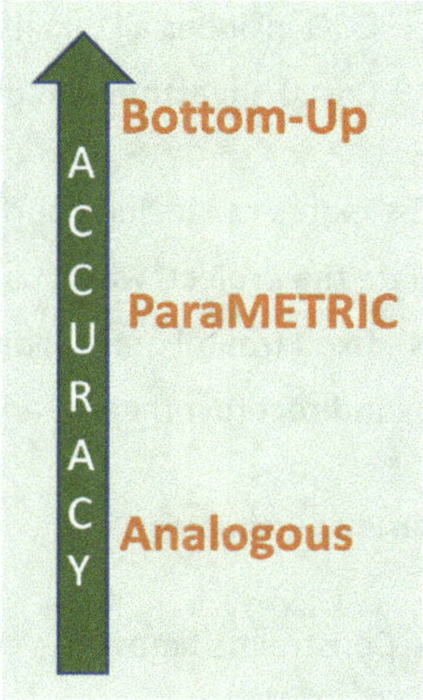

Figure 24. Project Estimation Accuracy

Parametric Estimating is the statistical relationship between historical data and other variables. Has higher accuracy, depending on the model's sophistication.

Bottom-Up Estimating is the method of estimating a component of work (i.e., work packages) rolled up with higher levels of the WBS for reporting and tracking. The size and complexity of the individual activity or work package influence cost and accuracy

Data Analysis

Alternate Analysis – Evaluate identified options to evaluate cost, schedule, resource, and quality impacts of buying versus making a deliverable.

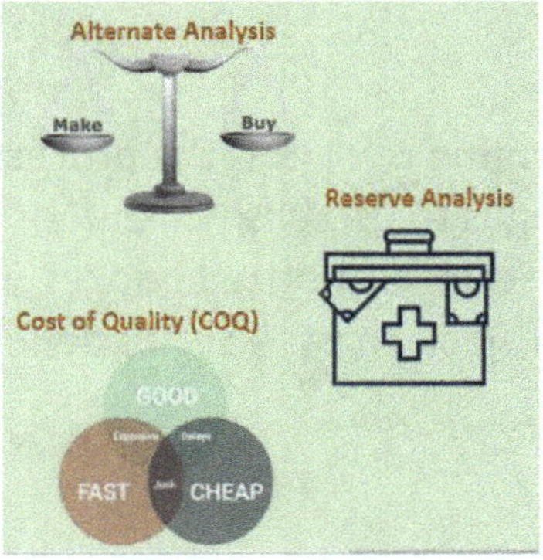

Figure 25. Project Data Analysis Methods

- Reserve Analysis- Contingency allowances/reserves (based on a fixed number, % of the cost estimate developed using quantitative analysis) are part of the funding requirements
- Cost of Quality (COQ) - Assumptions about COQ impact activity cost estimates

- COQ includes all quality-related costs over the life of the project (including REWORK = Failure Costs). Investment in preventing nonconformance to requirements.

Cost Estimates can include performing a quantitative assessment of probable costs of all resources to complete the project, which consists of the Variable (costs change as production changes - wages), **fixed** (rental of a building) , and the **Direct** (attributable to the project, travel), **Indirect** (overhead – administrative work) costs of the project.

The basis of Estimates can be documented, Range, and Confidence Level.

- Constraints (known)
- Assumptions
- Documents the basis, assumptions, and constraints
- Documents formulas used. Provides a range of accuracy (e.g., ROM, Budget, or Definitive)

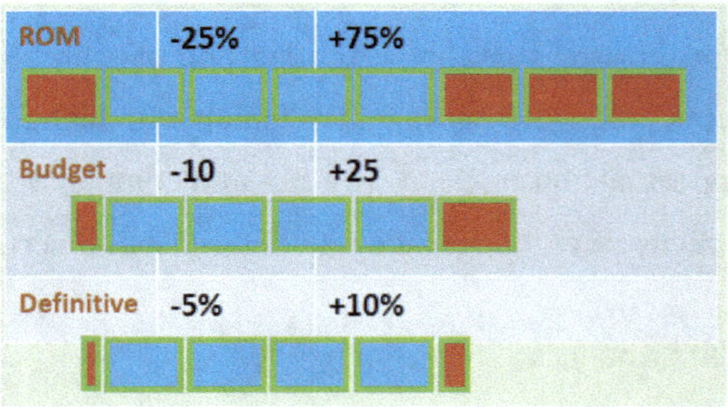

Figure 26. Basis of Estimates - 2

Determine Budget is the process of aggregating estimated costs of individual activities or work packages to establish an authorized baseline. Project cost performance will be measured against the authorized budget. The ability to influence cost is the greatest at the beginning of the project, so early scope definition is essential.

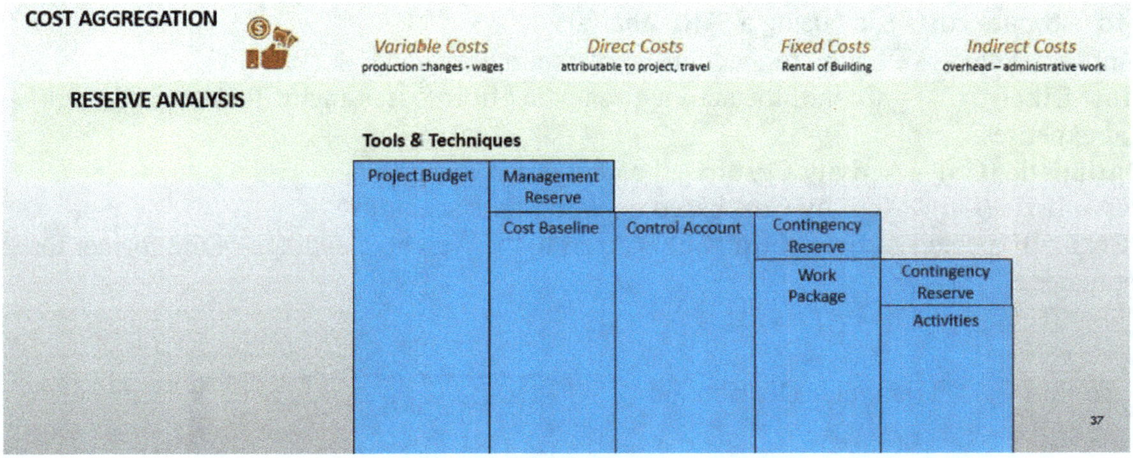

Figure 27. Budget Determination

Cost estimating & cost budgeting are so closely integrated that some view them as a single process; the PMBoK treats them as distinct processes (since the tools and techniques differ).

One way to estimate costs is by using a PERT Analysis

Three-Point Estimates - An Estimate that considers uncertainty and risk (PERT)

- **Most Likely (C_m)** – Cost of the activity, realistic effort 'assessment' for required work and expenses.
- **Optimistic (Co)** – Activity Cost based on best-case scenario
- **Pessimistic (Cp) -** Activity Cost based on worst-case scenario
- **PERT** = Expected Activity Cost (Ce) is equal to the weighted average of the former three estimates

Triangular Distribution

$$C_e = \frac{(C_o + C_m + C_p)}{3}$$

Beta Distribution

$$C_e = \frac{(C_o + 4C_m + C_p)}{6}$$

Figure 28. Pert Analysis - Three Point Estimating

Project Funding Requirements can include the total and periodic (quarterly, annually) funding requirements derived from the Cost Baseline. This baseline includes anticipated liabilities (known risks) and total budgeted funds (cost budget), which consists of the cost baseline plus management reserves (unknown risks).

Cost Aggregation is the process of rolling up the estimated costs of individual activities, work packages, and control accounts into project costs.

While Data Analysis Technique - Reserve Analysis includes:

(1) Contingency reserves, which are a part of the baseline
and

(2) Management reserves, which are a part of the project budget (not in the baseline), cover unplanned changes and unknown risks.

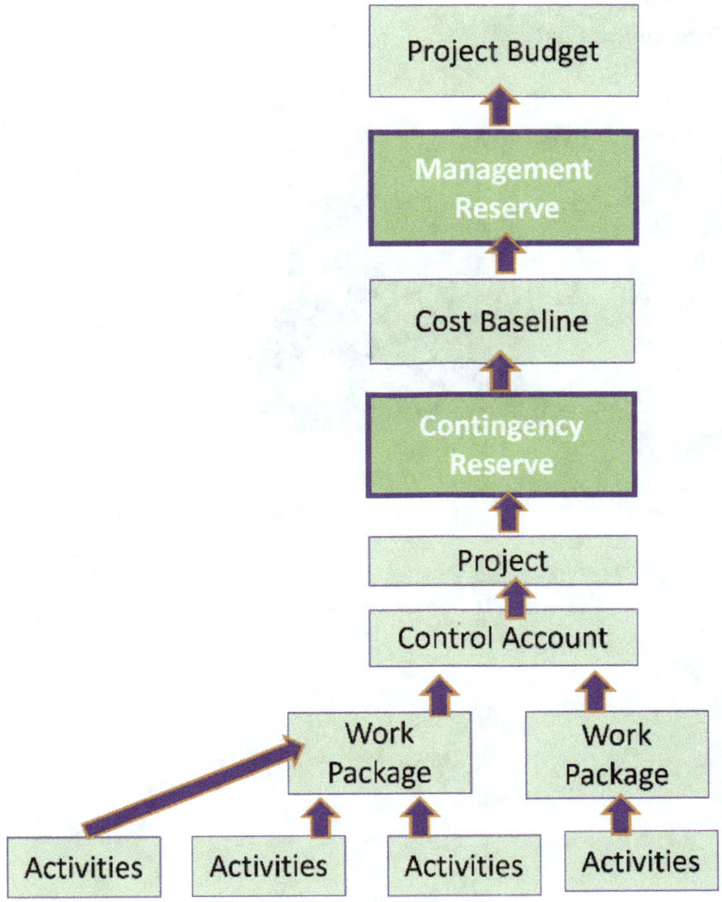

Figure 29. Project Cost Aggregation

Controlling Cost

How much did you say the project would cost?

ESTIMATED COSTS

How much did they give you to spend?

BUDGET AT COMPLETION

BAC

How much time do you have to complete the project?

PLANNED VALUE

PV

All of the planned tasks and activities accomplished a goal for the project – thus adding planned (or potential) value.

How much did they give you for unforeseen issues?

MANAGEMENT RESERVES – Remember this is you Ace-in-the-hole-money

Don't put in your budget.

There are several ways to calculate where you are at any given time in your project. PMI calls this Earned Value Management. It consists of many different formulas to calculate the projects:

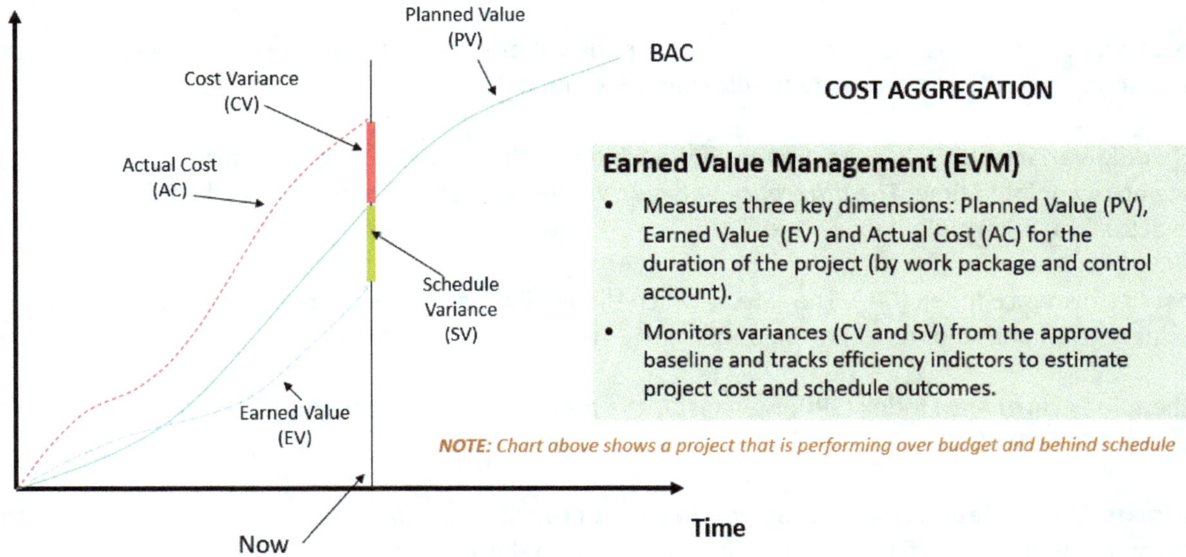

Figure 30. Earned Value Management Graph

Actual Costs (AC). Realized cost incurred for work performed during a specific time period. How much *money* was spent during a particular time period? No Formula: **Sum of expenditures for the time period**

Planned Value (PV). It measures the schedule constraint. It is the authorized budget assigned to scheduled work. How much work **should have been completed** at a point in time based on the plan? What is the estimated value of the work planned to be done? **Formula: PV = BAC x Planned % Complete**

Earned Value (EV). It validates the cost constraint. It is the realized cost incurred for work performed on an activity during a specific time period. How much is the value of the work completed during a particular period of time? **Formula: EV = BAC x Actual % Complete**

Actual % Complete. How much work ***has*** actually been completed as of **today**? Formula: **Actual % Complete = (actual hours to date/total planned project hours) x 100**

Cost Variance (CV). It is the amount of the budget deficit or surplus. The ***difference*** between what we expected to spend and what was actually spent. **Formula: CV = EV - AC**

Schedule Variance (SV). It is the amount by which the project is ahead or behind the planned delivery date at any point in time. The ***difference*** between where we planned to be in the schedule and where we actually are. **Formula:** SV **= EV - PV**

Cost Performance Index (CPI). The rate at which the project performance meets cost expectations during a given period of time. **Formula:** CPI **= EV / AC**

Schedule Performance Index (SPI). How fast is the project progressing compared to the project plan? Formula: SPI **= EV / PV**

Estimate At Completion (EAC). What we expect the project to cost based on where we are relative to cost and schedule. What are we forecasting to spend on this project?
Formula: EAC = BAC/CPI

Estimate to Completion (EAC). We are projecting how much ***more*** will be spent on the project based on past performance. **Formula: ETC = EAC – AC**

Estimate at Complete (EAC) Forecast predicts what you expect the total cost of the project to be			
Manual Bottom-Up Summation	**Budgeted rate**	**Present CPI (cumulative)**	**Current SPI and CPI (cumulative)**
• Original estimate is completely unrealistic or fundamentally flawed (aka "hitting the re-set button") • Bottom-up estimates (ETC) for remaining work are easy to obtain and are considered the most accurate predictor of future performance	• Variances experienced so far are not typical of what we can expect going forward *("atypical variances," "we can catch up since we are smarter now")* • Predicts all future costs at budgeted rate	• Project performance (cost variance experienced so far) will continue *("typical variance", "no variance" or "constant variance")* in future periods • Continue at same rate of spending	• Both schedule and cost efficiency rate matter (schedule impacts ETC) and will continue in the future • Assumes negative CPI and a fixed Project End Date
EAC = AC + (Bottom-up ETC) *Original estimate is flawed, need to use bottom up estimate for future performance.*	**EAC = AC + (BAC – EV)** *Cost Performance Index is flawed, so use future budget and earned value.*	**EAC = (BAC/ CPI)** *Cost Performance Index is good.*	**EAC = AC + ((BAC-EV) / (CPI*SPI))** *Schedule and Cost are critical, so use both schedule and cost.*

Figure 31. Project Estimate at Completion Forecasting

Variance at Completion. This is the difference between what was budgeted and what will actually be spent. It shows as over budget (negative) or under budget (positive). **Formula: VAC = BAC – EAC**

To-Complete Performance Index (TCPI). To stay in budget, what is the rate to complete the remaining work? The remaining work is the same (numerator: BAC-EV), but the funds remaining are different (denominator).

What do I need to do to maintain a steady course of performance? < 1 is good, greater than 1 is bad

TCPI for Budget At Completion (BAC)	TCPI for Estimate At Completion (EAC)
(BAC-EV) / (BAC-AC)	(BAC-EV) / (EAC-AC)
CPI is good (>=1.0) and work is performed at or above baseline plan	CPI is poor (<1.0) and risks, schedule and technical performance do not allow the PM to attain the BAC
PM continues working toward a viable (approved) BAC	PM must seek approval for new EAC

Figure 32. Project To-Complete Performance Index (TCPI)

The Project Stakeholders

The project manager must know who has an interest in the project. There will be internal stakeholders and external stakeholders on every project. Each of these individuals will have different interests and levels of power throughout the life of the project. The project manager must know all the players who will be affected by the project's life, as well as the project's outcomes or product.

Identify Stakeholders	Plan Stakeholder Engagement	Manage Stakeholder Engagement	Monitor Stakeholder Engagement
The major project stakeholders are identified prior to the project being incorporated. A project is initiated with the major stakeholders in mind.	Specifies how the project will interact with each stakeholder. It identifies and analyzes two items for each stakeholder: The level of interest the stakeholder has in the project, and their ability to control it. All stakeholder concerns are presented and analyzed to ensure the project is set up for success.	Ensures stakeholders are consulted to ensure their needs are met. Stakeholder interactions are executed according to the Stakeholder Management Plan, and changes to the plan are made, as necessary.	Executed on regular intervals throughout the project to assess the effectiveness of the Stakeholder Management Plan. reviewing stakeholder communications, gathering information about them, or even asking them directly how they feel about the project and/or their specific concern.

Figure 33. Stakeholder Management Phases

A larger plan that feeds the stakeholder management plan is called the communications plan. The communications plan will determine how each of these stakeholders will be communicated with throughout the life of the project. For our purposes, these two plans will be combined. The project manager must know who has an interest in the project. There will be internal stakeholders and external stakeholders on every project.

Identify your Stakeholders. The first step to any good stakeholder management plan is proper stakeholder identification. Stakeholder: An individual, group, or organization who may affect, be affected by, or perceive itself to be affected by a decision, activity, or outcome of a project, program, or portfolio.

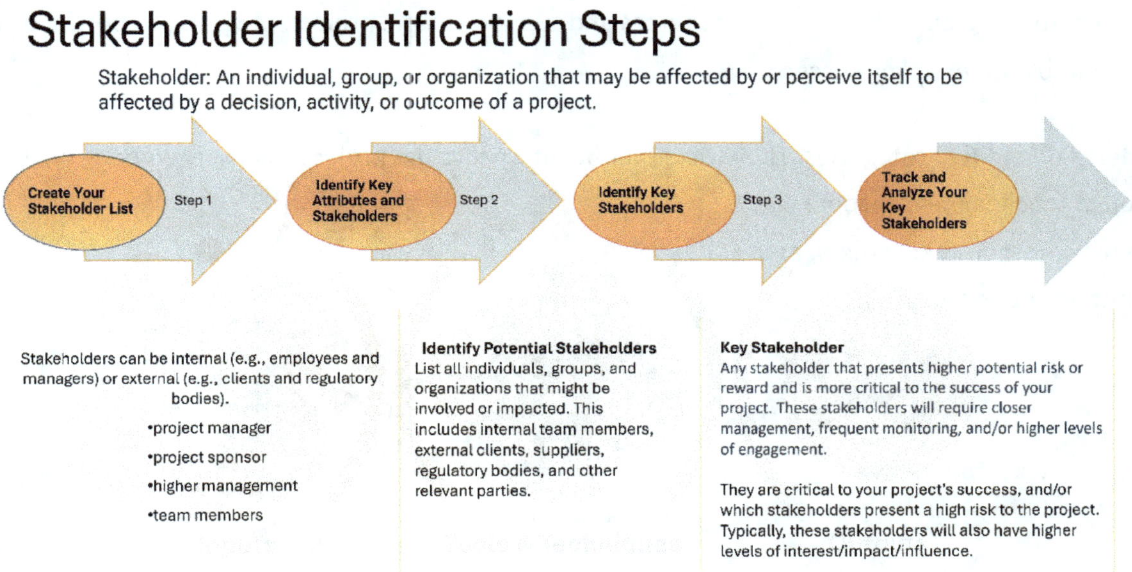

Figure 34. Stakeholder Identification Steps

Stakeholder Management: The stakeholder management plan is a subsidiary plan of the project management plan that defines the processes, procedures, tools, and techniques to effectively engage stakeholders in project decisions and execution based on the analysis of their needs, interests, and potential impact.

Agent: Active proponent(s) and driver(s) of the change.

Lead: The lead function supports the overall change management process and implementation, including coordinating associated work streams within the project's scope.

Recipient: A person directly or indirectly impacted by a change.

Sponsor: A person or group who provides resources and support for the project, program, or portfolio, and is accountable for enabling success.

Stakeholders fall into two categories. They will either be internal to the project – actively working on it- or the project touches them in some way; those are the external stakeholders, and they are just as important.

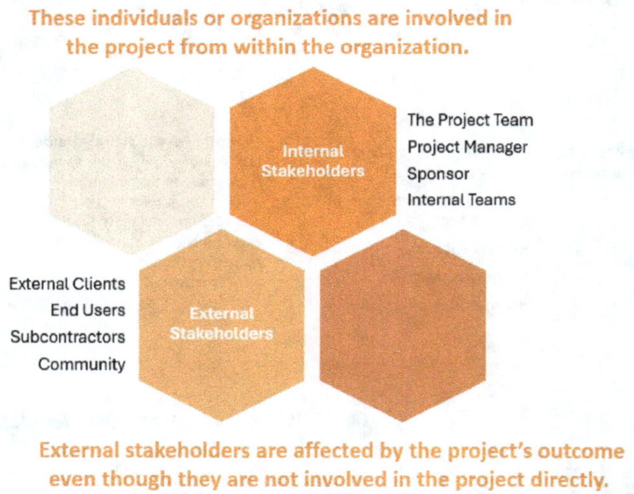

Figure 35. Internal and External Project Stakeholders

Prioritize Your Stakeholders. ...

Interview Your Stakeholders. ...

Unaware: At this level, stakeholders are not aware of the project and its potential impacts. They lack information about the project's existence, objectives, and potential benefits or drawbacks.

Resistant: Stakeholders are aware of the project but oppose it. They may actively resist the project (e.g., by campaigning against it) or passively resist (e.g., by withholding support or resources). The resistance could stem from a perceived negative impact on their interests.

Neutral: Stakeholders are aware of the project but neither support nor oppose it. They are indifferent and not engaged in the project's processes or outcomes.

Supportive: These stakeholders are aware of the project and its potential impacts, and they support it. They might provide resources, assist in overcoming obstacles, or endorse the project to other stakeholders.

Leading: At the highest level of engagement, stakeholders are not only supportive but also actively involved in ensuring the project's success. They might take on a leadership role, champion the project, and use their influence to promote its benefits and overcome challenges.

Ensure

Commitment of stakeholders at all stages of the project

Stakeholder expectations are met. The tools used could be negotiations and communication

Anticipate future problems and address potential concerns throughout the life-cycle of the project

Critical Points

Stakeholder influences are the highest at the start of the project and as the project progresses the influences continue to reduce

Project sponsors assistance to be taken by the project manager whenever required

Stakeholder mapping should be a dynamic process that enables organizations to represent all stakeholders visually, the political environment in which the project operates, and the relationships among them. Using "commitment to the change" on the x-axis and "influence" on the y-axis, this chart can facilitate discussion on how to manage key stakeholders. It may also be possible to group particular stakeholders and develop actions that are targeted at the group rather than specific individuals.

1. **Transparent Communication:** Transparent communication means being open and honest with your stakeholders. Share important information regularly and clearly so everyone knows what's happening. This builds trust and helps avoid confusion or misunderstandings.

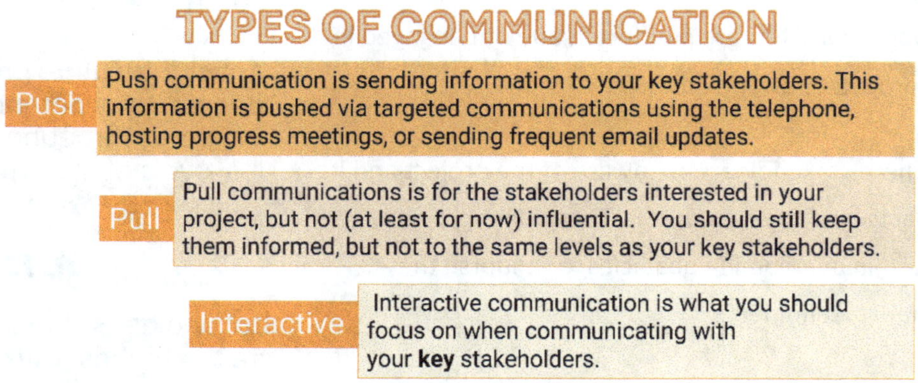

Figure 36. Types of Project Communication

2. **Consultation:** Consultation is about asking stakeholders for their opinions and feedback. It is important to listen to what they say and involve them in decision-making processes. This ensures they feel heard and valued in the project.

3. **Understanding Stakeholder Needs:** Understanding stakeholder needs means taking the time to learn what matters to them. Each stakeholder may have different concerns or goals, so it is important to know what they expect. This helps you address their interests effectively.

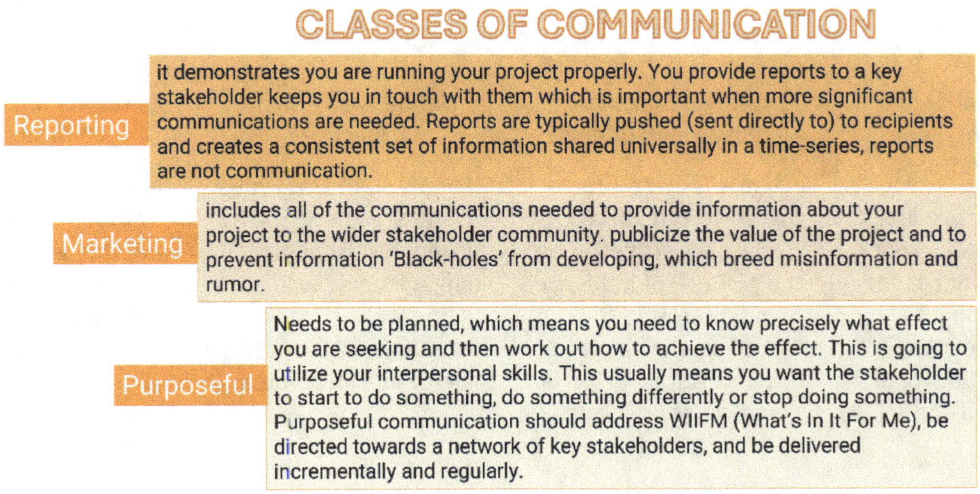

Figure 37. Classes of Project Communication

4. **Early Involvement:** Early involvement means engaging stakeholders from the very beginning of a project. When stakeholders are included early, their input can help shape the project's direction, and any concerns can be dealt with immediately.

5. **Building Relationships:** Building relationships with stakeholders is the key to long-term success. You must develop trust and mutual respect. Good relationships can help create strong project support and smooth over any problems that arise.

6. **Planning:** Planning is essential for effective stakeholder engagement. You must know how and when to communicate with stakeholders, what information they need, and how to keep them informed. A clear plan will ensure that no one is left out or surprised.

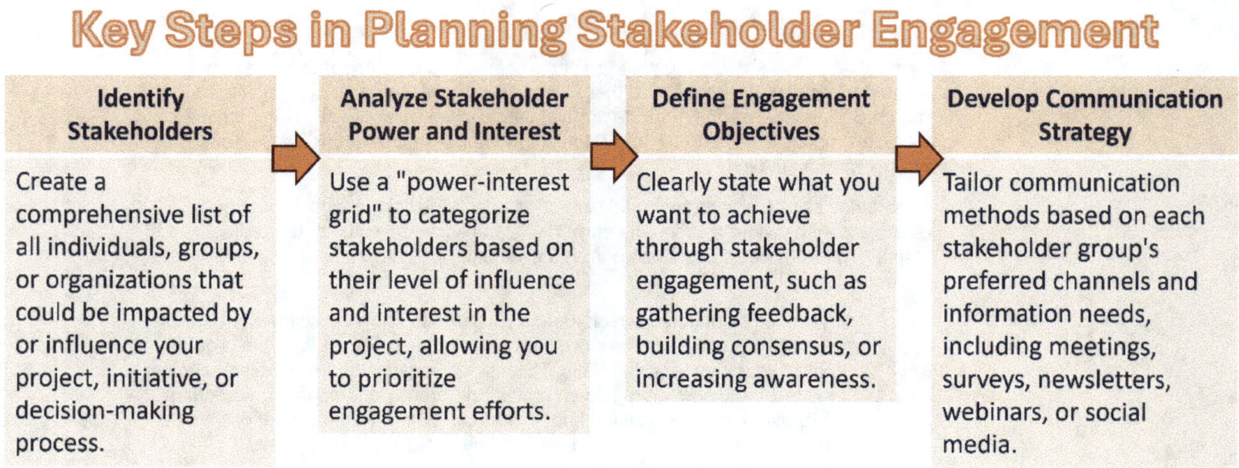

Figure 38. Key Steps in Planning Stakeholder Engagement

7. **Anticipating Challenges:** Anticipating challenges means thinking ahead about potential issues or conflicts with stakeholders. By identifying these early, you can develop solutions or strategies to prevent them from becoming bigger problems.

8. **Managing Risks:** Managing risks involves being prepared for any uncertainties that may affect the project. You should understand how stakeholders could influence these risks and work together to reduce the negative impact.

9. **Establishing Clear Expectations for Success:** Setting clear expectations for success helps everyone know what they are working toward. Ensure stakeholders understand their roles and expectations to prevent confusion and keep everyone on the same page.

10. **Measuring and Adapting Engagement:** Measuring and adapting engagement means checking how well your engagement strategies are working. Regularly assess stakeholder satisfaction and involvement, and be flexible in making changes to improve communication or collaboration if needed.

This process of communicating with and working with stakeholders to meet their needs/expectations, address issues as they occur, and build appropriate stakeholder engagement in project activities throughout the project's life-cycle is termed the Management Stakeholder Engagement process.

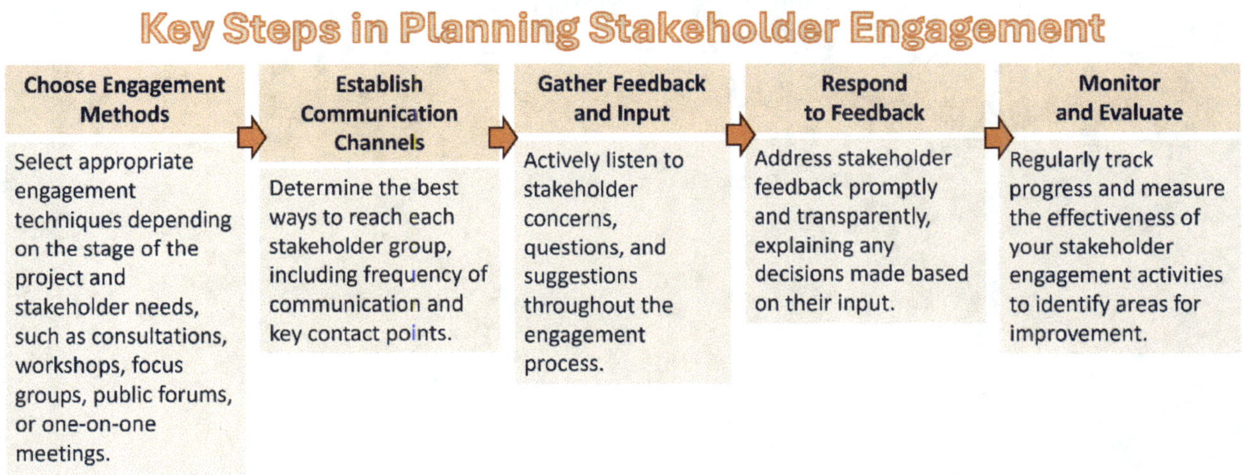

Figure 39. Key Steps in Planning Stakeholder Engagement

Monitoring stakeholder engagement includes assessing the stakeholder engagement strategy to ensure stakeholders remain engaged throughout the project lifecycle, including communication channels, engagement frequency, and methods for seeking input and feedback.

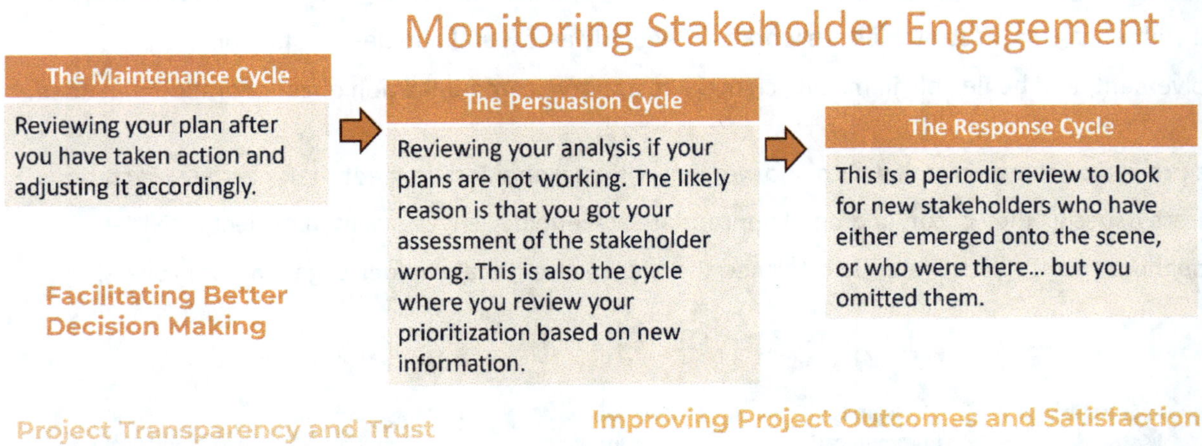

Figure 40. Monitoring Stakeholder Engagement

Risks and Issues

There are nine risks that most projects focus on. They are cost risk, schedule risk, performance risk, operational risk, market risk, governance risk, strategic risk, legal risk, and external hazard risk.

Risk Management Planning	Risk Identification	Qualitative Risk Assessment	Quantitative Risk Assessment	Risk Response Planning	Risk Monitoring & Control
The initial work performed to identify the risk management approach to be used on the program and the program-specific assessment criteria.	The process of actively identifying and documenting all potential threats and opportunities that could impact a project's success, essentially listing out all possible risks that might affect the project's deliverables, timelines, or budget during its execution	The process of evaluating and prioritizing potential project risks based on their likelihood of occurring and the potential impact they could have on the project, using subjective assessments like "high," "medium," and "low" to determine the severity of each risk.	The process of converting the impact of risk on the project into numerical terms. This numerical information is frequently used to determine the cost and time contingencies of the project.	Identifying the risk response strategy (ies) that will be used and the detailed risk response plan(s) (what will be done or not done) for each risk identified. Including identifying the trigger event that will cause the risk response plan to be executed.	Monitoring for a risk event occurrence, reassessing the risk (likelihood and consequence) and monitoring the performance of the risk response plan and reporting the results.

Figure 41. Risk Management Phases

Understanding project management, its phases, and management plans is essential before starting a project. Skipping any of these steps will almost ensure your project fails. In the early days of project management, before understanding the project lifecycle, phases, and the importance of management and sub-management plans, 80% of all projects failed. Most failed projects were due to poor planning and poor communication. Be sure to have all of your questions answered and your project plans created, reviewed, and signed by the project sponsor, and everyone is in charge of decision-making on the project. Everyone must understand the importance of being good stewards.

Identifying the risks on the project is by far the most labor-intensive of all of the steps in this process. It is where you pull out the interpersonal tools in your toolbox and work with the project team to bring in everything that could affect you as you move the project toward success. Subject Matter Experts (SMEs) are your best allies in this process. Through their experience, they have encountered risks you might not think of in a bubble. Lean on them in brainstorming sessions and make lists of those items.

This is the time to bring back the work breakdown structure. Go through each phase, milestone, and/or task, and ask them when previous risks occurred, what happened, how it happened, and what they did about it. Also, ask them about the triggers. How did they know they were coming? What are some things to look out for? How did they alert the PM in the past?

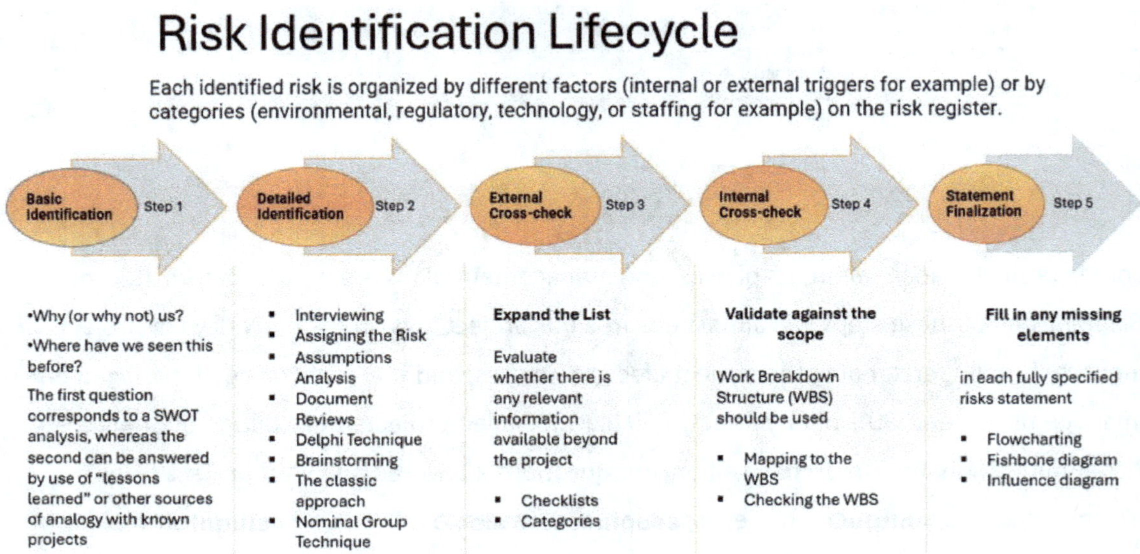

Figure 42. Risk Identification Lifecycle

This is also the time to assign those risks to the team members most likely to deliver the solution. Putting the people in charge of the risks within their areas of expertise, leveraging what they know and how they can help build the strategy to manage those risks, is a key element in successfully identifying project risk.

The next step is to perform a qualitative risk analysis of the risks you identified. The point is to prioritize individual risks by assessing their likelihood of occurrence (probability) and the severity they would have for the project if they occurred (impact). There are industry-standard methods to use when conducting this first-pass analysis of the project risks identified. They are as follows:

Delphi method
identifies and prioritizes the most important risks in a project and forecasts the likelihood of occurrence for each risk event, including their impact on project objectives. It involves experts' responses to a series of questions about the probability and impact of events. It involves experts' responses to a series of questions about the probability and impact of events. Each round takes place over several days or weeks, and experts often continue to submit their responses until the project manager has all the information they want.

Risk probability and impact assessment
Determines whether a risk is acceptable or unacceptable based on both its probability of occurrence and its potential severity if it occurs.

Bow tie analysis
identifies, assesses, classifies and develops mitigation strategies for a certain risk. This method gets its name because its analysis chart looks like a bow tie, and it helps identify the relationships between causes and effects. On one side is a list of things that may result in negative events, while on the other is a list of all consequences of the event. A bow tie analysis helps you develop strategies to eliminate those causes or effects.

Decision tree analysis
Identifying all possible outcomes of an event and assigning them numerical values. These values determine their likelihood of occurring, and the higher the value, the more likely the risk can occur. These values can guide you in choosing the most effective actions to reduce the risk.

SWOT analysis
A strengths, weaknesses, opportunities and threats (SWOT) analysis is a strategic planning method for evaluating the various components of a project and how they might affect its outcome. The analysis involves identifying the internal and external factors that are favorable and unfavorable to achieving the venture's goals.

Figure 43. Qualitative Risk Analysis Methods

Once you have performed a thorough qualitative analysis, the next step is to perform a qualitative risk analysis. This is the data you will use to build charts and a dashboard so risks can be viewed in a way most people can understand and make informed decisions. It is a process that helps managers numerically analyze how identified risks may affect a project's objectives and the contingency reserves required to account for them. This analysis is a big part of how you will develop strategies to address those risks.

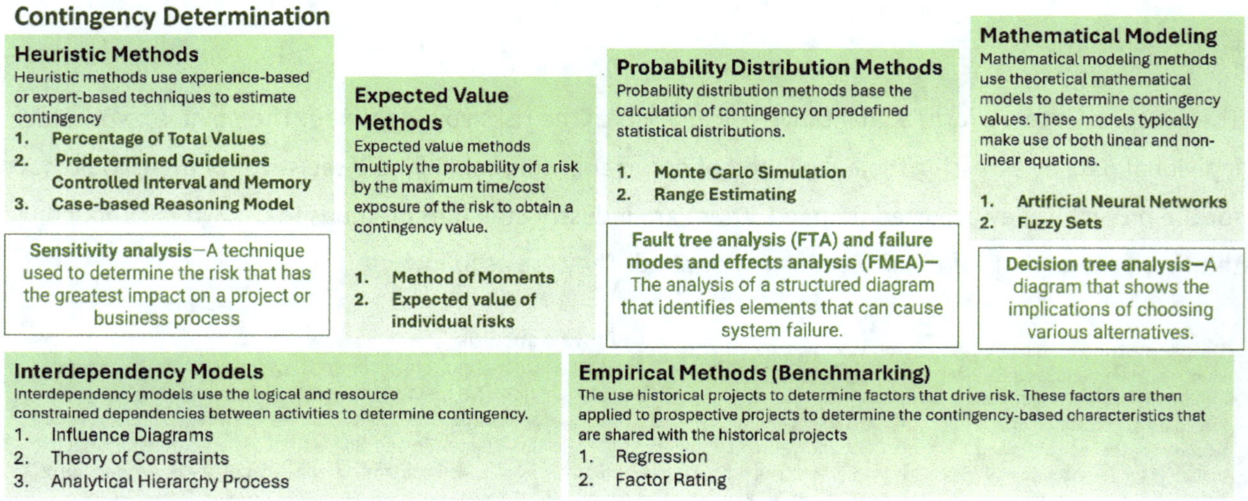

Figure 44. Risk Management Contingencies

The ways you handle the project's risks will guide the strategies you adopt and the responses you make. A risk response plan should include a definition of what is to be done, who will do it, the schedule, and how the work will be funded. The options for dealing with risk are: (1) Avoid or eliminate the risk by pursuing a completely different approach to the task, thus eliminating the risk. (2) Transfer the risk by moving the risk elsewhere (to a supplier, to an insurer). (3) Mitigate the risk by developing a plan to reduce the consequence and/or the likelihood of a risk event occurring. (4) Accept the risk by allowing the risk to remain and dealing with the consequences if it happens.

PMI.org has specific ways to handle risk that include (5) Exploiting the risk by "...ensuring that an opportunity occurs". In these instances, the project manager may delay, avoid, or activate specific project activities to increase the probability of a risk occurring. (6) Sharing the risk by taking "...ownership of an opportunity to a third party who is best able to capture the benefit for the project." Tapping into a partner to share the risk is a strategy to increase the possibility that the positive risk

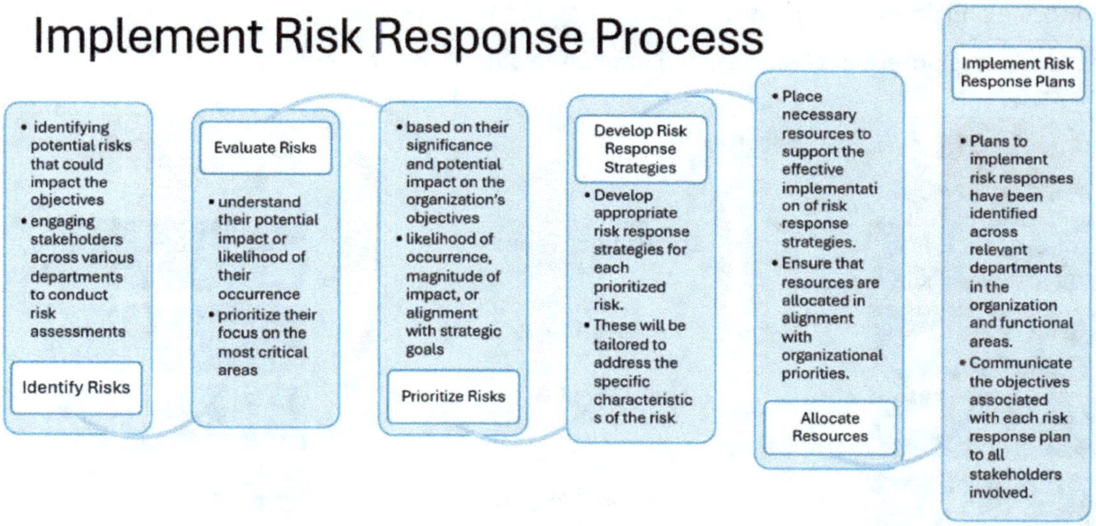

occurs to everyone's benefit. Or (7) Enhancing the risk, the opposite of eliminating risk, enhancement

Figure 45. Implement Risk Response Process

increases the possibility of occurrence. PMI defines enhanced risk as the work to "...increase the probability of occurrence or impact.".

Be watchful for trigger conditions or signs that a risk event has occurred and be prepared to implement the response strategy immediately. Remember, not every risk needs to be mitigated; consider other options for managing project risk. Remembering cost management, risks were budgeted earlier. You very well may need to update your budget at this point to reflect the new information you have uncovered. Risk needs to be balanced with cost and schedule.

EXECUTION, MONITORING, AND CONTROLLING

During the execution phase, the project manager and the project team carry out the work defined in the project schedule, working on tasks and activities and completing the milestones that form the phases. In the monitoring and controlling phase, the project manager actively reviews the project's status as it progresses, evaluates potential obstacles, and implements necessary changes.

Figure 46. Execution Phase Steps

The Project Team

Procurements

Costs

The Project Schedule

Risks and Issues

Communications

Project Quality

Integrated Change Control

Figure 47. Monitoring and Controlling Phase Steps

Executing the project, monitoring all aspects of the project, and controlling to bring all elements into line or make changes happen in chorus, even though they are broken into separate phases.

Scheduled Project Work

When executing the work outline in the project schedule, you would have assigned each item a start date and a finish date, which, in turn, would calculate the time the task should take to complete. Also, if you have completed network diagramming, you will have pinpointed the predecessors and plugged them in. While the project team is busy finishing their tasks, you check their progress regularly. As this is the monitoring phase, you will take the information you are collecting (performance information), plug it into your schedule tracking system, and start to make decisions as to how to proceed in controlling the project.

	EXECUTION		MONITORING	CONTROLLING	
SCHEDULED WORK | TASKS	A Scheduled Task Starts in accordance with the Project Schedule	Work task from the project schedule is be completed by the project team	Work Performance is being gathered on resources, time, etc. *Percentage Completed* are being tracked. cost expenditures are being calculated	The work on the task finishes earlier than the state on the project schedule	Close work item earlier than the *Finished Date* and start new work *earlier* than the original *Start Date*

Figure 48. Scheduled Work and Tasks in Execution, Monitoring, and Con

There are a lot of people doing a lot of different things right now, and establishing a routine for gathering your project data is a must. During the monitoring phase, you must determine, based on the work and timelines, how often you should check in and how the work is progressing. Using the monitoring data, you will decide how to progress through your project schedule.

Including whether some tasks will take more time than planned, or some that will finish early, and other work will need to be started early. This is the absolute nature of the execution phase.

Resource Management

During the planning stage, the work was assigned to the appropriate project team member based on their skills and availability. Resource management balances the two elements—skill and availability —throughout the execution, monitoring, and controlling phases. Availability is usually a pain point for projects. Remembering that the project is a temporary endeavor, and that the resources are too. Those who are working on the project have 'day jobs'.

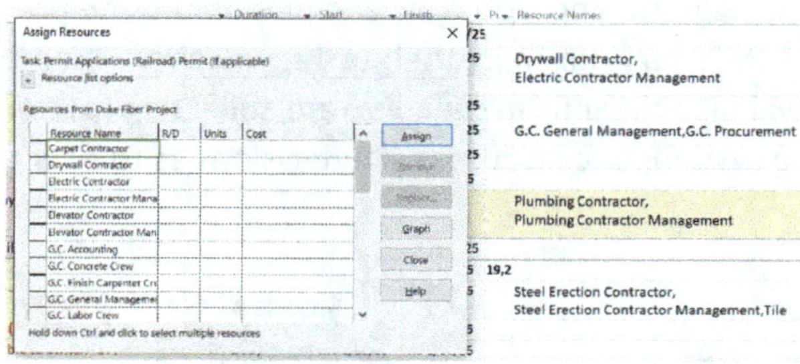

Figure 49. Assigning Project Resources - 1

They are often lent to projects in addition to their regular work. Understanding their time needs to be planned deliberately, and swings or changes to their availability may not be possible.

	EXECUTION		MONITORING		CONTROLLING
RESOURCES	The resource (Pam) assigned to the task starts to completed the task assigned	Pam is very skilled and is completing the faster than anticipated	From the updates received it looks like Pam will finish the task early	Pam finishes the task and needs more work or will leave the project to do work of their own	Give Pam the next task that can be completed according to the project plan

Figure 50. Resources in Execution, Monitoring, and Controlling

When tasks require more time or additional resources, they occur in the monitoring phase, and making decisions about where to allocate your human resources requires constant monitoring. When tasks are completed early, it is imperative that they be closed and new work be assigned to replace them, to make the most of the time we have with our borrowed resources, especially if they bring special skills to the project.

Communications Management

Communicating with Stakeholders includes the project team, executives, unit managers, and the project team itself. There are many modes and channels of communication, and many of them are used simultaneously during the execution, monitoring, and controlling phases of a project. Receiving and sending out updates on project performance is the main project management task. Others include giving and receiving feedback on performance measures; updating and sending project status updates; following up on inquiries made within and outside the project team; and ensuring inter-team communication is unobstructed and transparent.

	EXECUTION		MONITORING	CONTROLLING	
COMMUNICATIONS	The manager of the development team (Leo) only wants the weekly summary of the project updates	Leo retires and Dan replaces him as the new manager	Reach out to Dan to find out his project communication needs and impact	Dan wants to be included in all project updates, including status meetings and reports	Update the stakeholder register to replace Leo with Dan and communication channels

Figure 51. Communication in Resources in Execution, Monitoring, and Controlling

There are many others used to monitor communication levels and ensure that stakeholders receive information about the project's progress in the manner and at the time they require it. When communication channels and modes change, you, as the project manager, must make the necessary updates to realign communication.

Risk Management

The risk management lifecycle is the foundation for managing risks throughout the project. Grooming the risk register and monitoring risks include checking in with the project team to ensure that the triggers identified during the planning phase have not occurred. A regular risk and issues review should be in place. This can happen during regular project meetings or regularly scheduled risks and issues meetings.

	EXECUTION		MONITORING		CONTROLLING
RISKS & ISSUES	A risk from the registry has triggered and needs to be addressed	The risk is discussed at the weekly risk management meeting	A mitigation plan is put in place.	The steps to mitigate the risk are underway and being tracked	The risk does not roll up into an issue and is closed

Figure 52. Risk and Issues in Resources in Execution, Monitoring, and Controlling

The lifecycle includes discussing the risks that could affect the work currently being executed. It is the project manager's responsibility to monitor for potential dangers at the time and to ask the right questions of the project team to solicit their input on whether they foresee any risks. When a risk trigger is pulled, it should be addressed via an initial discussion, prioritized, and the plan put in place should be reviewed against the current landscape.

The conversation around that risk includes how the risk or failure is presenting itself, the causes that initiated the trigger, and then what will be done about it. And then, of course, as you are in the execution phase, you will put the plan for that risk into play. The last step is to continue monitoring the execution of the risk plan so it does not escalate into an issue. If the plan addresses the risk, you will then update and close that risk.

Procurement Management

Procurements are being purchased and delivered at this time. It is the responsibility of the project manager to ensure that the resources required for the project are ordered, paid for, and delivered in accordance with their necessity and the project schedule.

Many things can go awry in procurements, so the project manager must ensure that orders are placed properly and that packages are tracked and delivered on time.

	EXECUTION		MONITORING	CONTROLLING	
PROCUREMENTS	The scanners for the upcoming deployment have just been ordered and an invoice is submitted	The business office will process the invoice for payment.	Ensure you receive an update on when the payment was made and the vendor received it	Track shipment to ensure the equipment will arrive on time	Close the procurement of the scanners

Figure 53. Procurements in Resources in Execution, Monitoring, and Controlling

When deliveries are delayed or not delivered at all, substitutes may need to be made, extra costs for faster delivery may need to be paid, or alternate vendors may need to be reached out to to get the project what it needs, when it needs it.

Quality Management

Deliverables are being created in accordance with their definitions of done during the execution phase.

Ensuring that the work or items being delivered meet the expected quality standards sometimes falls to the quality team. Still, ultimately, it is the project manager's responsibility to establish a system or procedure for inspecting and approving all work items, milestones, etc.

EXECUTION			MONITORING	CONTROLLING	
QUALITY	Quality levels are set for work items	As the work is being completed the quality is reviewed when possible	Testing or review of the work item is compared against the quality standards set	During the review it is determined the work item does not meet the set quality standards	The work item is failed and sent for rework

Figure 54. Quality Management in Resources in Execution, Monitoring, and Controlling

Consistently monitoring work through demos and review sessions ensures that those responsible for quality have time to review, submit feedback, rework completed work, and achieve eventual approval.

PROJECT CLOSE

Once the project's activities, tasks, and milestones are completed, the project will enter a project close phase. During the project close phase, all activities, tasks, and milestones are checked to ensure they are completed according to the plan, accepted by the sponsor, and in good working order.

Figure 55. Project Close Phase Steps

The project manager should hold a final project closure meeting with the Project Sponsor, Project Owner, and the entire Project Team. At the project closure meeting of a normal/successful project close, the questions that should be answered are (1) did we accomplish the objectives of the project, in other words, did we fulfill the scope of the project? (2) Where do the fruits of this labor go from here? (3) What do we do now?

As we know, not all projects close successfully, and the type of closure depends on the kind of project closure being undertaken. During premature, failed, or change-in-priorities project closures, the team should be informed of the reason for the premature end and their next steps. In many cases, the project team is disbanded, and the time dedicated to the project is reallocated to another project or returned to their regular work full-time.

Formal Acceptance of Project Deliverables: Closing the project includes receiving formal sign-off from the project sponsor that the project's final product is being successfully delivered. Verification that the scope of the project has been fully executed and is of acceptable quality. A formal document stating this is created, and the appropriate signatures are collected for inclusion in the closure report.

Closing Procurements: Closing out a project also requires that all the bills have been paid. This includes attending to all claims, paying all invoices, closing all contracts, and resolving any outstanding issues.

Lessons Learned: The project manager should conduct a lessons-learned meeting with the project team. This is often rolled into the final project closure meeting. When documenting lessons learned, the team will share their experiences, successes, and challenges.

When going through what could have been done better, the problem–impact–resolution process is often used successfully.

Transition of the Final Product: In most cases, the final product will be handed over to the customer as a finished item or moved into operations. Transferring the system into operations or delivering it to the sponsor officially ends the project. All that is left to do is make our final project management updates and archive the project!

And after all that, we celebrate!

CHAPTER THREE: AGILITY BUILT-IN

Agile is a mindset, not a prescription. It is a holistic way to approach project management that goes far beyond tools, techniques, and templates.

In this chapter, you will learn:

- What is Agile & Why Should We Use It?
- Agile Methodologies
- A Shared Vision of Agile
- Adaptive Planning
- Continuous Improvement

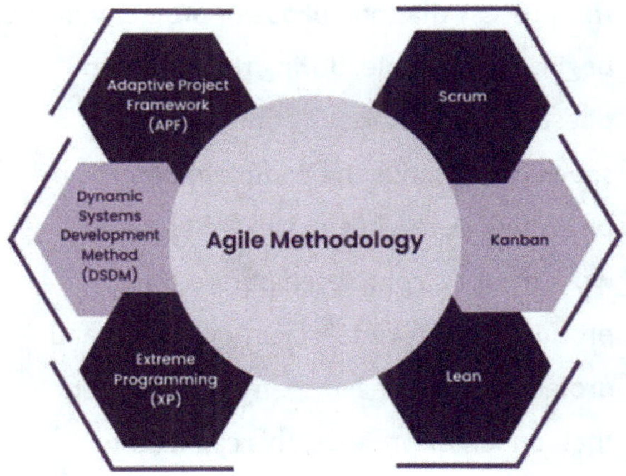

The project management process does not have to be linear. In fact, most projects these days aren't. They are a series of loops of design development, demonstration, and handoff. The project has adapted to new ways of working, including dispersed teams and shorter time-to-adoption. It is clear that the shrinking time-to-market for technology has pushed projects to much shorter timelines and more frequent functionality additions as new options routinely become available.

The linear project process is called traditional, or waterfall (predictive), project management. It is during this process that one phase of project management must be completed before the next phase can begin. For example, during the initiation phase, all project requirements and specifications must be complete before any project work can begin. Next, all project work must be completed before the product is reviewed. Project managers and project sponsors have seen over the years that, on larger projects, this can lead to outdated requirements and a lack of flexibility to add or update previous requirements.

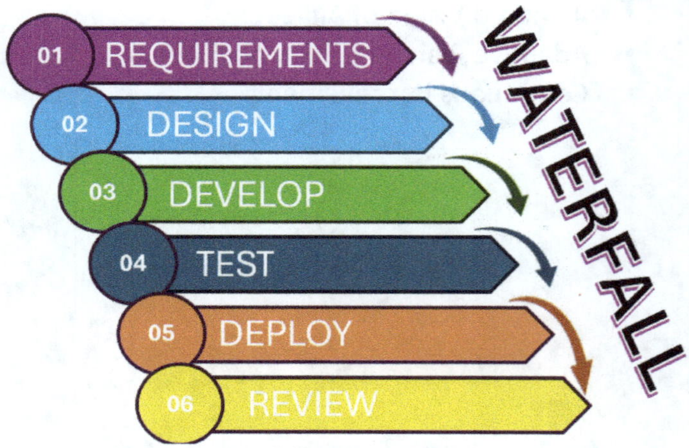

Figure 56. Waterfall Project Methodology

The five stages of the waterfall (predictive) method are all important and must still be undertaken. That is not what agile has come to replace. Instead, it's another way of accomplishing these same goals, allowing for changing requirements, new ideas, and new ways of working as a team.

Agile project management requires a mindset that prioritizes agility at all times, through all phases, in all communications, and in all work. When working this way, the project instead moves through the waterfall (predictive) stages continuously, using minor incremental improvements to create small, frequent releases. This allows the project team to move through the work more intelligently and, most times, faster, with better returns on time and effort, because you are working toward agreed-upon goals that make sense of the reality on the ground.

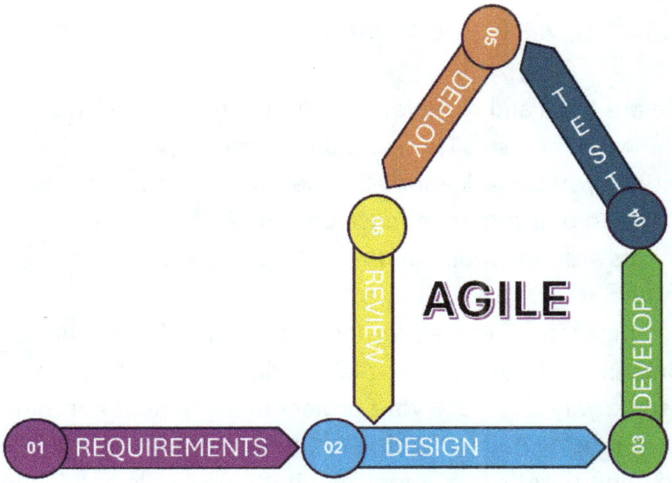

Figure 57. Agile Project Methodology

BEING AGILE VERSUS DOING AGILE

There are tools and techniques that many teams pull from the Agile toolbox, but they are not delivering on the Agile mindset. There is a difference between doing Agile and actually being Agile. There are some questions you can ask yourself to see which team you belong to. These questions are based on the declaration of interdependence and the Agile Manifesto. If you study what these two foundational elements are demanding of the agile team, you will be in good shape.

Delivering faster and creating less documentation are not agile; they are shortcuts many teams implement and call 'hybrid agile'. Having a mix of Agile and Waterfall (predictive) practices is an awesome way to ensure your project management approach is tailored to your organization's needs. However, using Agile to get rid of the part of project management you don't like or that holds you back is 'no bueno'. Let's take a look at what Being Agile and Being Agile looks like:

Figure 58. The Agile Toolbox

Declaration Of Interdependence

In 2001 and again in 2005, the pioneers of Agile gave us the six principles they coined the phrase 'Declaration of Interdependence' of Agile Project Management.

Table 2. Declaration of Interdependence Founders

DAVID ANDERSON

SANJIV AUGUSTINE

CHRISTOPHER AVERY

ALISTAIR COCKBURN

MIKE COHN

DOUG DECARLO

DONNA FITZGERALD

JIM HIGHSMITH

OLE JEPSEN

LOWELL LIDSTROM

TODD LITTLE

KENT MCDONALD

POLLYANNA PIXTON

PRESTON SMITH

ROBERT WYSOCKI

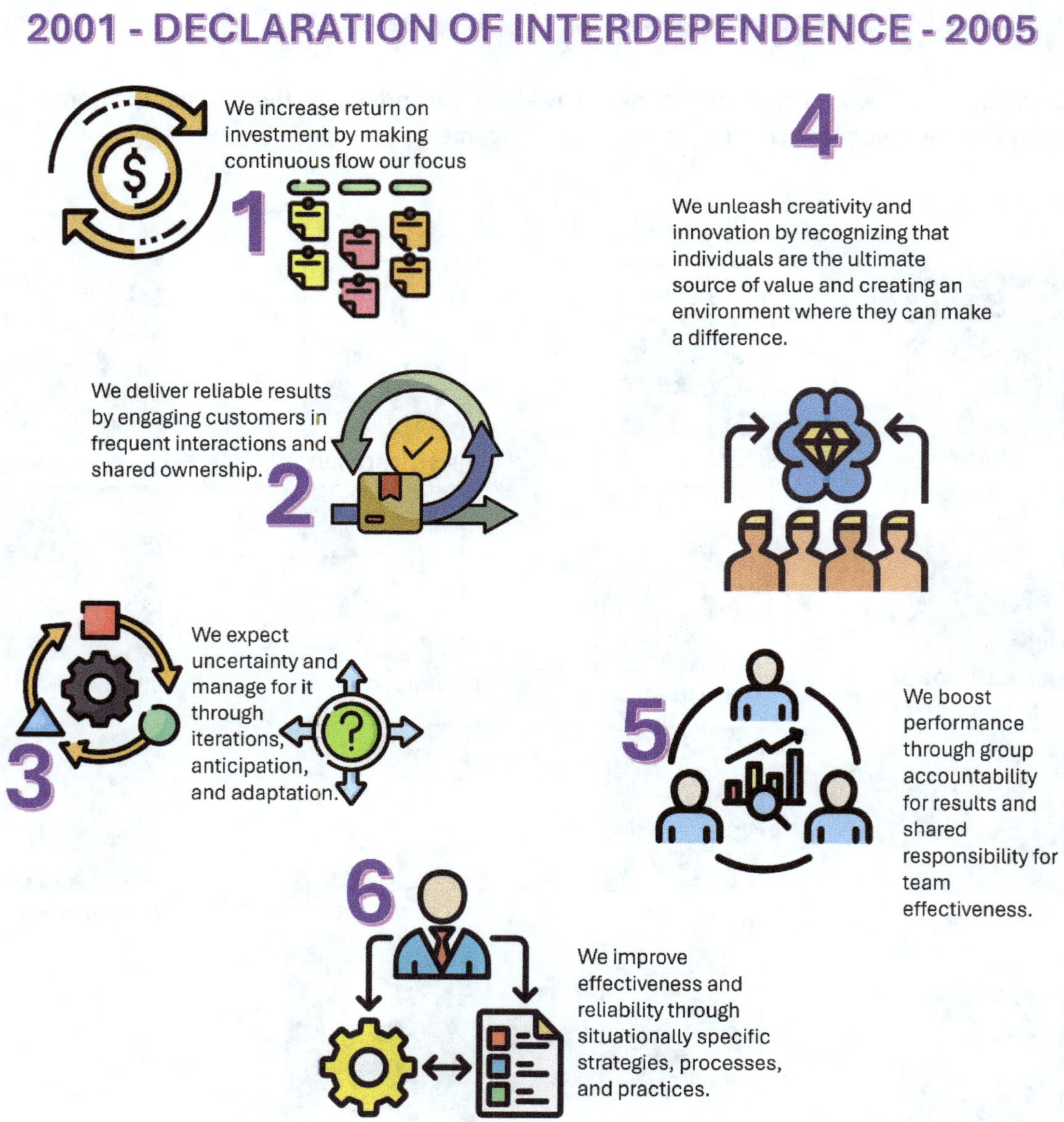

Figure 59. Declaration of Interdependence

The Values of the Agile Manifesto

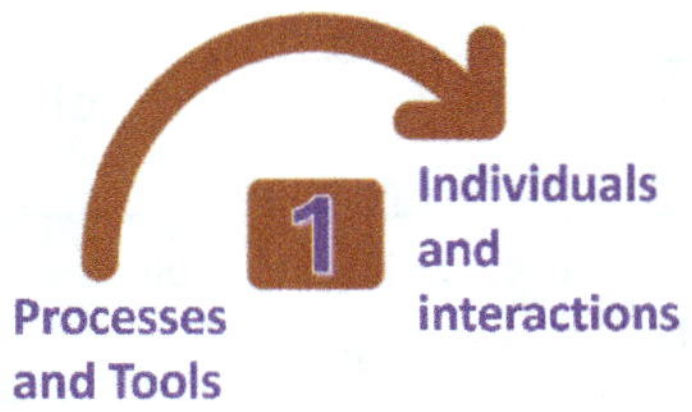

Individuals and interactions over processes and tools: Adherence to strict tools and processes that hinder forward progress is the wrong answer. Open, frequent, and transparent communication with the project team and stakeholders goes a long way toward delivering the work on time and to the highest quality standards.

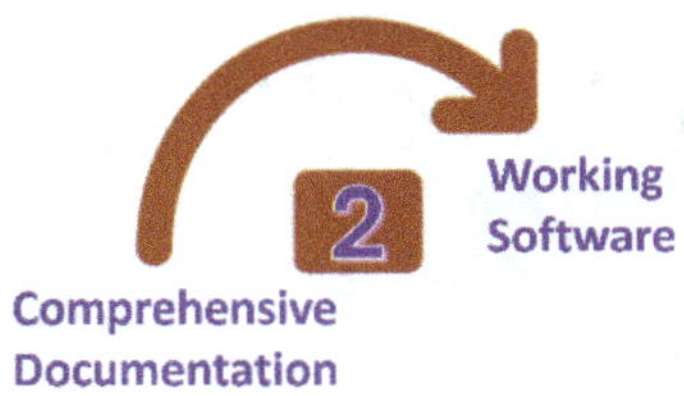

Working software over comprehensive documentation: Documentation for documentation's sake is not part of the recipe for successful projects. Of course, the documentation required to fulfil regulatory requirements is essential and should be completed as prescribed. This is a better way forward, not a shortcut.

Customer collaboration over contract negotiation: Coming to an agreement about the 'thing' —what it should look like, how it should function, how it should be built —is best achieved when those invested in its success talk it out.

Responding to change over following a plan: Take the time to look at where they are, and what needs to be done, and then make the right decisions for the current reality. Following a premade plan has its place and should not be disregarded. The question can evolve into: Using Agile, how can we improve the plan?

The 12 Principles of the Manifesto Adapted for the Trifecta

Table 3. The 12 Principles of the Manifesto adapted for the Trifecta

1	**Our highest priority is to *satisfy the customer* through the *early and continuous delivery* of valuable software.**	
	The goal of a project is to deliver the scope. The highest priority, then, would be to ensure that the project's scope is delivered on time, within budget, and of the highest quality. That is the Agile frame, and within those borders is the method of delivering continuously toward that goal. Focusing on demonstrating to the customer smaller releases through frequent releases with shorter cycle times of a minimum viable product or a product with minimal marketable features to build on.	✓ Minimum Viable Product (MVP) ✓ Minimal Marketable Feature (MMF) ✓ Frequent Releases ✓ Cycle Time ✓ Throughput ✓ Small Releases ✓ Scaling Practices ✓ Demos
2	***Welcome changing requirements*, even late in development. Agile *processes harness change* for the customer's competitive advantage.**	
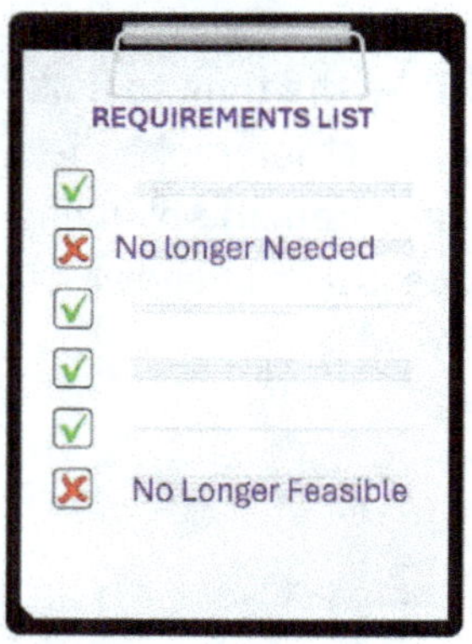	Building on #1, the project team will use the *feedback* from the demonstration reviews to *elaborate* on what should come next. These *learning cycles* are used to tailor the product and the process, refine the initial requirements with new, better information, improve the next iteration, and refine and adjust the requirements backlog to move more meaningful work into the next iteration to serve the customer and their business needs better.	✓ Progressive Elaboration ✓ Learning Cycle ✓ Process Tailoring ✓ Feedback Methods ✓ Approved Iterations ✓ Risk-Adjusted Backlog ✓ Backlog Refinement ✓ Change for Free ✓ Prune the Product Tree

3	***Deliver* working software *frequently*, from a *couple of weeks to a couple of months*, with a preference for the *shorter timescale*.**

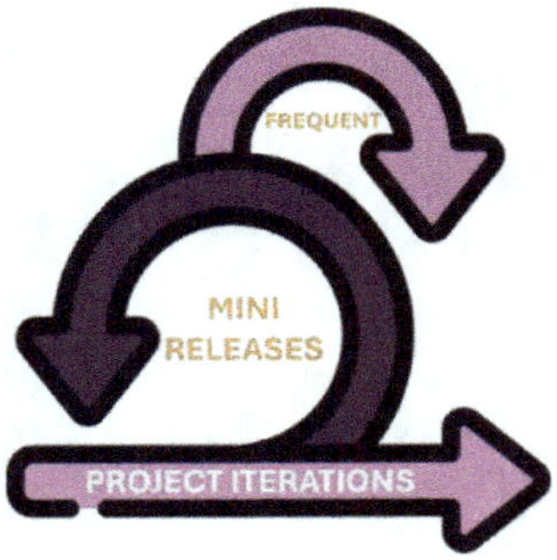

Building on #'s 1 and 2, utilizing planning in rolling waves of designing, testing, building, and demonstrating an MMF or an MVP, the project team increases the opportunities for the customer to verify and validate the work. Utilizing short-term development cycles or iterations, ranging from a couple of weeks to a month, allows targeted work to be in progress at any time. These shorter cycles or iterations also enable more accurate lead-time calculations, leading to better forecasting of ideal times. It also ensures consistent throughput towards the product and ensures that the team is focusing its efforts on the right work.

- ✓ Minimal Market Feature (MMF)
- ✓ Minimal Viable Product (MVP)
- ✓ Work in Progress
- ✓ Workshops
- ✓ Ideal Time
- ✓ Lead Time
- ✓ Throughput/Productivity
- ✓ Reviews
- ✓ Frequent Verification and Validation
- ✓ Rolling Wave Planning
- ✓ Iterations

4 **Business people and developers *must work together daily* throughout the project.**

The cross-functional agile project team is composed of a diverse group of individuals who bring their specialties and abilities to a specific endeavor. Interactions such as meetings of many types are the keys to its success. Interpersonal relations are the foundation of this success. Active listening and the elements of emotional intelligence are required for fruitful interactions to move the work forward in a positive way. Agile offers many interactive tools and techniques to bring the team together to discuss and plan the work. Teams meet in daily standups and planning meetings to refine the backlog and plan the next iterations, provide feedback during demonstrations, and participate in retrospectives to review and adjust for the next iteration. There are many opportunities for interaction in Agile throughout the project.

- ✓ Product Feedback Loop
- ✓ Retrospectives
- ✓ Intraspectives
- ✓ Coaching and Mentoring
- ✓ Emotional Intelligence
- ✓ Active Listening
- ✓ Daily Standups

5	Build projects around ***motivated individuals***. Please give them the ***environment and support*** they need, and ***trust them*** to get the job done.

Empowering the project team through trust and self-governance. The agile team, made up of the right people with the right skill sets, now requires the trust and space to move through Shu-Ha_Ri.

Shu (守 - "to keep," "obey"), when the team is formed and the roles, responsibilities, and work are clearly defined and strict. Everyone has very defined lanes and is learning how they will interact within these confines. Ha (破 - "to break," "detach") is when the good work starts. It is during this time that the team relies less on the lines that divide them and more on open, frequent communication, as referred to in #4. Finally, there is Ri (離 - "to separate," "leave"), where the team becomes high-performing, utilizing osmotic communication, relying on intrinsic motivators, and building on a foundation of servant leadership to get the project work done.

- ✓ Emotional Intelligence
- ✓ Servant Leadership
- ✓ Intrinsic Motivation
- ✓ Extensic Motivation
- ✓ Team Motivation
- ✓ Adaptive Leadership
- ✓ Coaching and Mentoring
- ✓ Osmotic Communication
- ✓ Team Space
- ✓ Workshops
- ✓ Tuckman, Drefus, Shu-Ha_Ri Models

6	**The most efficient and effective *way to convey information within and to* a development team is a *face-to-face conversation*.**

Agile offers many opportunities for the project team to prioritize direct, real-time communication. One of the foundations of agile is the types and frequencies of the meetings throughout the project management life cycle. Agile meetings encourage product owners and developers to *communicate in real time* about the product, requirements, refinements, conflict resolution, and *retrospection*. They encourage team members to work in close proximity to one another (*collaborative team spaces*) actively listen to one anothers professional opinions (*intraspectives/ backlog grooming sessions*), review there hard work (*demonstrations*), hear teir views on how to proceed (*planning meetings*), how the work in proceeding (*daily standups*), and how they performed and how it can be improved (*retrospectives*).

- ✓ Active Listening
- ✓ Daily Standup Meetings
- ✓ Collaborative Backlog
- ✓ Grooming Sessions
- ✓ Sprint Planning Meetings
- ✓ Frequent Demos
- ✓ Pair-programming
- ✓ Collaborative Team Spaces
- ✓ Co-located Teams
- ✓ Conflict Resolution
- ✓ Focused Listening
- ✓ Internal Listening

7 *Working software* is the primary measure of progress.

There is no doubt that many key performance indicators (KPIs) are used to measure a project's success. Agile reminds us that all those metrics and any earned value become noise to success if the product the customer approves of is not the result. Not to say that performance information is not essential, because it certainly is. A fail-fast mentality means moving forward even in times of uncertainty and testing ideas rapidly. The point here is that designing and releasing *minimum viable features* rather than fully developed features to build toward releases is the most reliable predictor of a project's success. Delivering the scope —the outlined product — is the point—the only point of the project. Everything else falls under process—not success.

- ✓ Productivity
- ✓ Minimal Market Feature (MMF)
- ✓ Minimal Viable Product (MVP)
- ✓ Earned Value
- ✓ Throughput
- ✓ Information Radiator
- ✓ Fail Fast
- ✓ IKIWISI

8	**Agile processes *promote sustainable development*. The sponsors, developers, and users should be able to *maintain a constant pace indefinitely*.**

Agile projects require the team to find and maintain a sustainable pace throughout the project. Short, succinct iterations are the foundation for finding and keeping this pace throughout the project. To create this pace successfully, teams must keep a few things top of mind. The first is to set realistic goals that the team can achieve within the time available. As part of this determination, it is essential to remember that this is a cross-functional team, and its members have responsibilities in their respective units. Agile provides tools such as work-in-progress limits (WIP), cumulative flows, and burndown charts to keep an eye on what is actually achievable. As of course, making course corrections whenever needed.

- ✓ EVM for Agile Projects
- ✓ Cumulative Flow
- ✓ Diagrams
- ✓ WIP Limits
- ✓ Value Stream Mapping
- ✓ Control Limits
- ✓ Risk Burndown Graphs
- ✓ Variance Analysis
- ✓ Trend Analysis
- ✓ Empirical Processes

9 *Continuous attention* to *technical excellence* and *good design* enhances agility.

Technical excellence includes ensuring that the team is not only agile but can evolve with technology and the changing requirements and expectations of the customer. Paying as much attention to the non-functional requirements (e.g., performance and reliability) as to the functional requirements used to build the product. Keeping a finger on the pulse of the project's behavioral aspects allows the seasoned professional to see around corners and spot trouble triggers. During this time, when projects are more closely aligned with organizational strategy, technical excellence is imperative to remain aligned with the organization.

- ✓ Adaptive Planning
- ✓ Pre-mortem
- ✓ Retrospectives
- ✓ Prioritizing Value
- ✓ Process Cycle Efficiency
- ✓ Process Tailoring
- ✓ Technical Debt
- ✓ Consistent Value
- ✓ High Standards
- ✓ Adaptation
- ✓ Nonfunctional Requirements (NFRs)

10 *Simplicity* – the art of *maximizing the amount of work not done* – is essential.

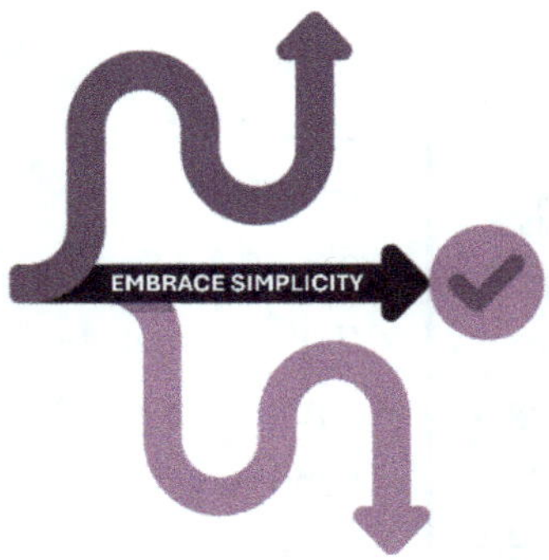

We have all heard the adage: "Work smarter, not harder." In part, that goes to the heart of work simplistically. Doing the work that needs to be done, in other words, prioritize the most essential and critical tasks and push those that are not as critical or non-essential to the bottom of the list. The key to working simplistically is not adding extra complexity to the work. No gold plating, automating tasks that are tried, true, and repetitive. The Pareto Principle reminds us that 20% of our efforts account for 80% of our results.

- ✓ MoSCoW
- ✓ Leading Metrics
- ✓ Minimal Viable Product (MVP)
- ✓ KPIs
- ✓ Pareto Rule
- ✓ Low-fidelity prototyping
- ✓ Non-value Added Time
- ✓ Pre-mortem

11 The best architectures, requirements, and designs emerge from **self-organizing teams.**

Once you have completed the work outlined in #5, the next step is to trust the project team to get the work done most efficiently and effectively. Each member within the scope of their abilities should feel empowered to make the best decision or work in front of them. Each member should feel like a servant leader – leading from the middle. At this point, individuals should feel intrinsically motivated and have developed the interpersonal skills in #6 to communicate effectively and share knowledge and experiences, forming a flat project team that gets the work done.

- ✓ Empowered Teams
- ✓ Co-location
- ✓ Engagement
- ✓ Ethics
- ✓ Expert in Earshot
- ✓ Knowledge Sharing
- ✓ Internal Listening
- ✓ Interpersonal Skills
- ✓ Motivation

12 At regular intervals, the team **reflects** on how to become more effective, then **tunes and adjusts** its behavior accordingly.

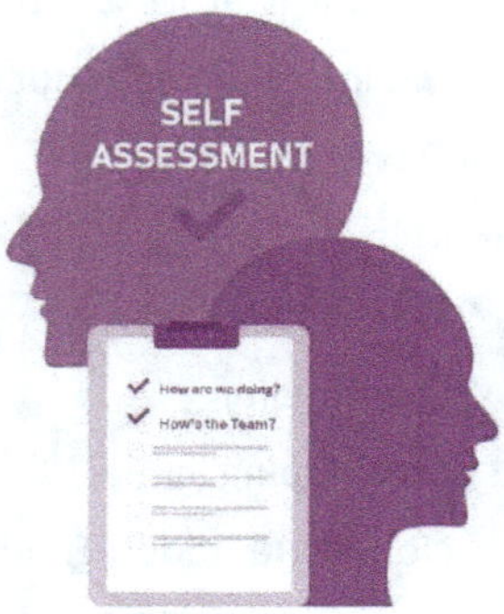

Continuous improvement is the foundation of Agile. It is why the work is broken into small increments, to fail faster and learn quicker. It is the reason for the different planning meetings: to understand the work in front of us – the work is worth doing. It is this goal of continuous forward movement that drives intraspectives before we start and retrospectives after we finish. Creating a specified time in the project life cycle to discuss what went well, what didn't go so well, and where the process can be tweaked to improve things in the future is being agile!

- ✓ Adaptation
- ✓ Adaptive Leadership
- ✓ Intraflection
- ✓ Retroflective
- ✓ Gulf of Evaluation
- ✓ Intraspectives
- ✓ Continuous Improvement

AGILE LIFECYCLES

There are four different ways to approach the project life cycle. Each defines a specific path to the project's finish line. The work is very similar; it's the paths through the work that vary.

1. A **predictive life cycle** is also commonly known as the waterfall approach to project management. It is also referred to as the traditional approach because it was the initial project management process introduced by the United States military to get big, complex things done. It makes sense: when they need to know the budget, time, and resources upfront, planning the work before it ever starts reduces the uncertainty and complexity, allowing project teams to sequence predictable work. Using this life cycle ensures that firm requirements are in place, thereby reducing the project's risk.
2. An **iterative life cycle** approaches the project using feedback loops. This approach allows the project team to succeed or fail fast and learn fast to improve the next iteration.
3. An **incremental life cycle** uses a set time to complete testable work while moving towards larger and, of course, the final deliverable.
4. **Agile life cycle** combines the iterative and incremental approaches to design, build, and test work frequently.

AGILE METHODOLOGIES

Agile comprises principles, values, tools, and techniques that, when used, improve the project management process. By leveraging the project team, stakeholders, flexibility, iterations, and the basics of the project management life cycle, agile serves as a methodology of methodologies. Several methodologies use the Agile Framework. Some are more popular than others. I am sure you have heard of Scrum, Kanban, Scaled Agile Framework (SAFe), Feature Driven Development (FDD), and Lean Software Development (LSD), but have you ever experienced some lesser-known methods like, eXtreme Programming (XP), Adaptive Project Framework (APF), Dynamic Systems Development Method (DSDM), Adaptive Software Development (ASD), Crystal and even Scrumban. In the article, What Are The Most Popular Agile Methodologies in 2025? (https://www.parabol.co/blog/most-popular-agile-methodologies/), The top 5 agile methodologies are being used in some fashion on projects: (1) Scrum – 87% (2) Kanban – 56% (3) Scaled Agile Framework (SAFe) – 53% (4) Scrum of Scrums – 28% and (5) Scrumban – 27%. These rankings are based on the most recent State of Agile Report (https://digital.ai/resource-center/analyst-reports/state-of-agile-report/).

Scrum Methodology

Scrum is a framework within the agile methodology that structures the project management process, inspired by the scrum in rugby. The focus is on teamwork. How the team works, learn, fails, and succeeds as one. The scrum framework is described as a heuristic because it assumes the team is in a continuous learning mode. Their experiences lead the team and evolve by adapting to what they learn in each iteration. The team learned to fail fast, learn, and evolve.

Key Ceremonies

Table 4. Agile Key Ceremonies

Backlog Grooming/ Refinement	Sprint Planning	Sprint
Daily Scrum or Stand Up	Sprint Review	Sprint Retrospective

Backlog Grooming/ Backlog Refinement

Get the right work done by focusing on the right things at the right time.

Table 5. Backlog Grooming/ Backlog Refinement Steps

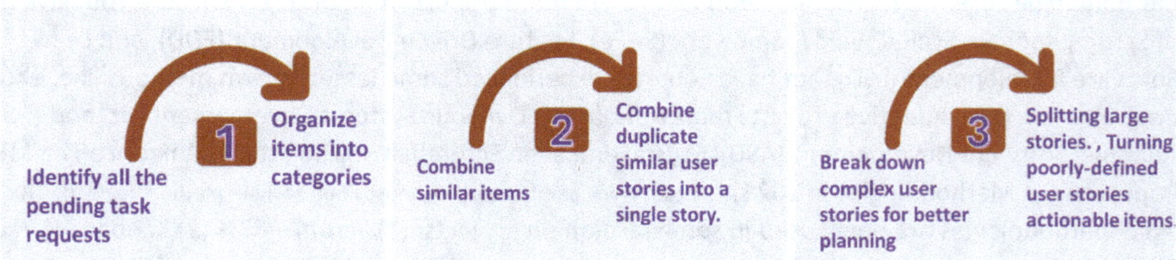

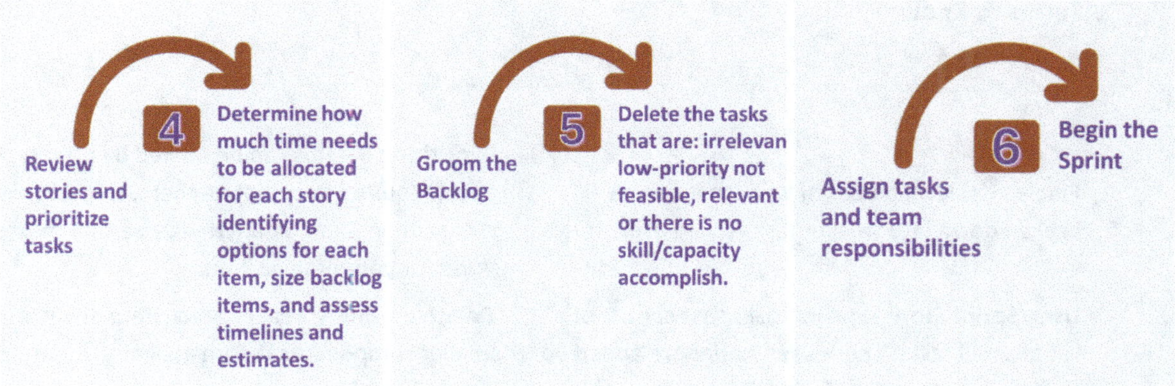

What is it? What is the goal? A product backlog is a list of tasks or requirements that need to be completed during the project. Grooming or refining the backlog is a hygiene effort. Its goal is to eliminate any waste in the requirements, thereby delivering value. During this activity, we take the time to weed out tasks that aren't essential to our immediate product delivery. By taking the time out to do this weeding, we ensure that the focus is on work that matter most and delivers the most value. It also underpins resource, risk, and time management. Helps us allocate resources to the right activity, thus reducing the risk of technical debt and keeping our product roadmap in check.

When does it happen? This meeting should take place midway through a sprint. Remember, we need the grooming completed and the following list ready to move to In Progress when the current sprint ends. It is best if it is a recurring meeting on the same day, at the same time, each revolution. This way, the team has a chance to prepare for the meeting properly.

How long does it take? Your meeting shouldn't run longer than 1 hour. Teams often use the 20/30/50 rule, which states that a fruitful refinement session should take no longer than 20% of the team's capacity, last no more than 30 minutes, and be limited to 50 story points.

How to prepare for the meeting? Before the backlog grooming session, review the backlog items on your own and familiarize yourself with the who, what, and why. Make sure you have a prioritized list of user stories and epics that you have input on during the review.

Terms to Know

Table 6. Scrum terms to know

Epic – high-level bodies of work that can be broken down into smaller tasks called user stories.	**Prioritizing – I**tems can be ranked by priority, the effort required to complete them, the risk involved in executing them, or anything else that makes sense for your organization.
User/Sprint Stories: major tasks that consist of a list of small tasks. These user stories are added up to form a larger body of work known as an epic.	**Relative sizing** - breaking each item down into smaller components before assigning them a size — small, medium, or large.
Features – A service or function of the product that delivers business value and fulfills a requirement. A feature is broken down into several user stories.	**MoSCoW prioritization technique -** Must-have, Should-have, Could-have, and Won't-have was created by product marketing specialist Dai Clegg in 1994

Sprint Planning: Sprint Goals, Team Velocity, Team Capacity. Sprint planning begins with a meeting during which team members review the project backlog and determine which items they'll tackle in the upcoming sprint.

Table 7. Sprint Planning Steps

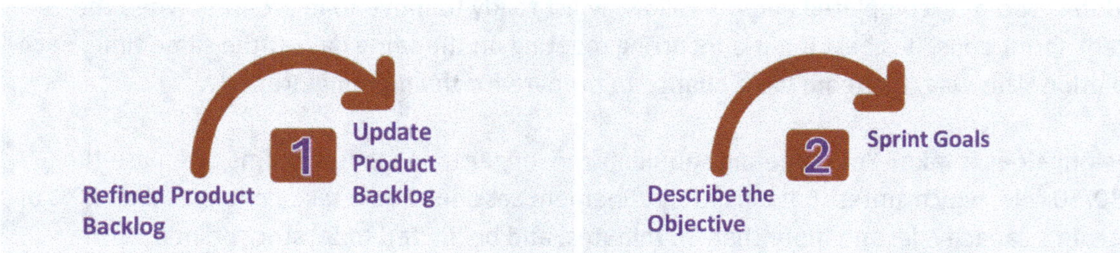

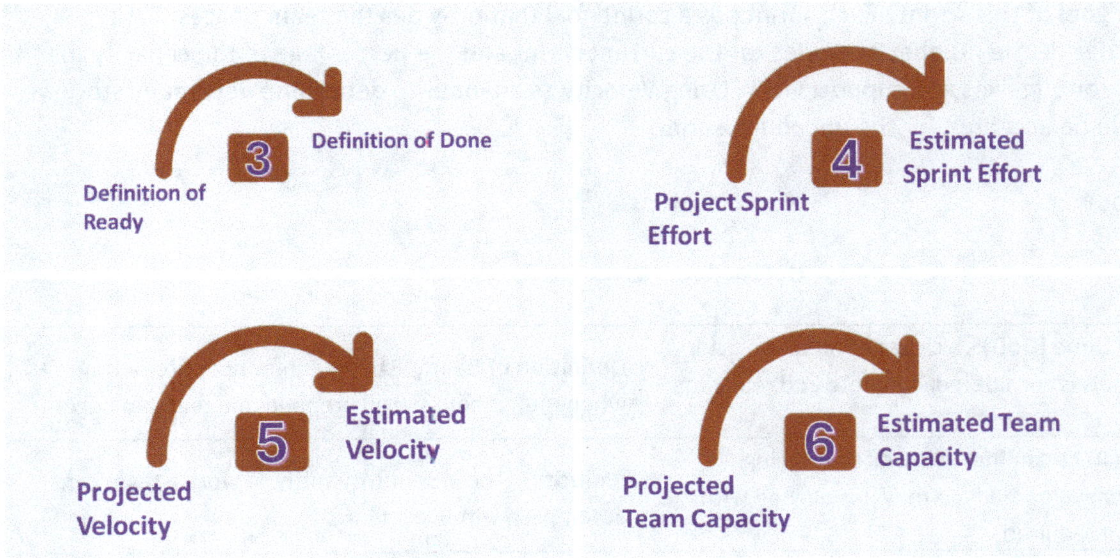

What is it? The team will prioritize the tasks and backlog you should deliver in the upcoming sprint. This will be done by setting priorities and goals and choosing the features that need to be added or upgraded in the upcoming sprint.

When does it happen? Planning is conducted before the sprint starts. If sprints last 2 weeks, then the planning meetings are also every two weeks. Planning meetings usually have two sessions. In the first session, the items to be built during the next sprint are selected. In the next session, an identification of tasks to support them is developed.

How long does it take? Usually, teams choose a two-hour-long planning session for a one-week sprint. The first is selecting the work, and the second is planning the tasks. The time set aside for sprint planning depends on how long and involved your sprints are. Sprint planning is timeboxed to 2 hours per week of the Sprint, so for a 2-week Sprint, it is one event for a maximum of 4 hours, and for a 4-week Sprint, it's one event for a maximum of 8 hours, and so forth.

What is the goal of this sprint? Each sprint has a sprint goal that provides the team's focus. Task planning to decide the number of stories for the current sprint and the percentage of the capacity that will be used for bug fixes and support work. Using Velocity as an input to determine how many story points should be accepted for the upcoming sprint.

Terms to Know

Table 8. Sprint Planning Terms to Know

Definition of Done (DoD) - a clear definition or criteria that, when met, is considered complete and ready for demo.	**Definition of Ready** - An agreement or criteria that, when met, is considered prepped and ready to begin
Just In Time (JIT) Planning – Accurately aligning planning and development so they it is aligned with when they are required.	**Velocity** – The amount/quantity of work a team can accomplish within a sprint.
Low-hanging Fruit – Tasks that require minimal effort to implement while delivering value.	**Timeboxing** - The maximum time allowed for the team to accomplish a task; there is no minimum time allowed.
Task Board & Burndown – Charting the work to be done, especially the amount of work/time remaining in the sprint/iteration.	**Swarming** – A collaborative approach (Multiple team members) to completing the development of a feature or a story.
Technical Debt – Exchanging speed to delivery over quality.	**Stretch Objectives** – Using realistic expectations, comprises tasks a team plans to do, but cannot commit to.

Sprint

What is it? A time-boxed period of time used by the project team to deliver chunks of work defined and placed into progress during sprint planning.

The Current Two Week Sprint Daily Schedule

The Sprint cycle is two calendar weeks, ten business days. There are Sprint Planning Activities and previous Sprint activities schedules along with the current Sprint activities.

Day One *Monday*	Day Two *Tuesday*	Day Three *Wednesday*	Day Four *Thursday*	Day Five *Friday*
PO & BA – Stand Ups	PO & BA – Stand Ups	PO & BA – Stand Ups	PO & BA – Stand Ups	PO & BA – Stand Ups
QA – Stand Up; Smoke Test of QA Environment	QA – Stand Up; Regress Previous Sprint	QA – Stand Up; Regress Previous Sprint	QA – Stand Up;	QA – Stand Up
Arch – Stand Up; Dev Support	Arch – Stand Up; Dev Support	Arch – Stand Up; Dev Support	Arch – Stand Up; Dev Support	Arch – Stand Up; Dev Support
Dev – Stand Up; Coding; Daily Build	Dev – Stand Up; Coding; Daily Build	Dev – Stand Up; Coding; Code Review Daily Build	Dev – Stand Up; Coding; Code Review Daily Build	Dev – Stand Up; Coding; Daily Build

Day Six *Monday*	Day Seven *Tuesday*	Day Eight *Wednesday*	Day Nine *Thursday*	Day Ten *Friday*
PO & BA – Stand Ups	PO & BA – Stand Ups	PO & BA – Stand Ups	PO & BA – Stand Ups	PO & BA – Stand Ups, Demo Planning
QA – Stand Up	QA – Stand Up	QA – Stand Up	QA – Stand Up	QA – Final Demo Testing; Integration Support
Arch – Stand Up; Dev Support	Arch – Stand Up; Dev Support	Arch – Stand Up; Dev Support	Arch – Stand Up; Dev Support	Arch – Stand Up; Demo & Integration Support
Dev – Stand Up; Coding; Code Review; Daily Build	Dev – Stand Up; Coding; Code Review Daily Build	Dev – Stand Up; Coding; Daily Build	Dev – Stand Up; Tech Debt & Bug fix; Daily Build	Dev – Stand Up; Code Freeze; Daily Build

Sprint planning creates capacity for each team member's responsibilities:
Sprint Planning, Current Sprint Activities and Post Sprint Product Deployment Retrospective

Figure 60. 2-week Sprint Planning Schedule. *https://images.app.goo.gl/htLBt4MduifksHp39 | https://slideplayer.com/slide/16979875/*

When does it happen? The sprint begins once sprint planning has commenced and the work for the time-boxed duration has been solidified.

How long does it take? A sprint is typically time-boxed for a month or less. Usually, sprints are scheduled in 2-week increments, but have been as short as a week. The sprint length depends on the project's complexity and the project team's preference. It is during the sprint that the project team actually completes the tasks and activities to produce a 'thing'.

Daily Scrum | Stand Up | Standups | Check-ins

Figure 61. Iteration Daily Standup

What is it? A standup is a daily meeting where the project team comes together to discuss three things: What did you complete yesterday? What are you working on today? Are there any roadblocks getting in the way?

While this might seem like an annoyance to some of your team, these meetings are essential for fostering the kind of communication that drives Agile project management.

When does it happen? Daily.

How long does it take? A 10–15-minute meeting.

Sprint Review

What is it? The team takes the time to review and demonstrate the work completed during the sprint. The review of the features developed to gather feedback on what was created and, of course, to ensure continued alignment with the requirements.

When does it happen? The sprint review takes place at the end of the sprint.

How long does it take? The review is typically limited to a few hours —1 hour per week during the sprint's duration, with a maximum of 4 hours total.

Sprint Retrospective

What is it? An opportunity for the project team to learn and grow by reflecting on: How did the Sprint go? Did the process work for us? Did we use the right tools?

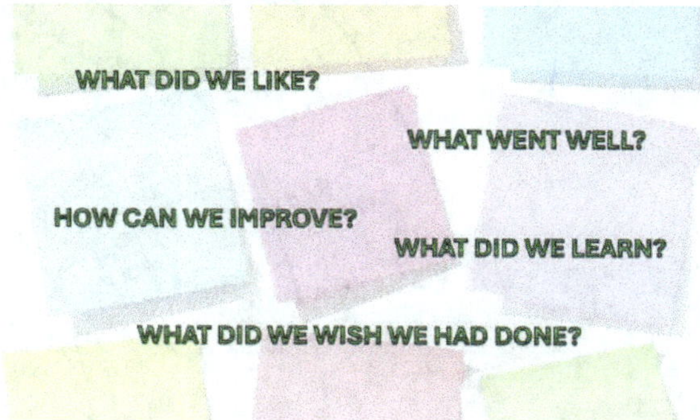

When does it happen? The retrospective should take place after each sprint ends.

How long does it take? The entire team should spend at least 30 minutes asking and answering retrospective-relevant questions.

How to prepare? Come up with your own answers. Review the answers, prioritize the list based on what is important to the team, then develop an improvement plan and share it with the team.

Kanban Methodology | The Agile Board

Using Kanban and task boards has been a popular method for managing projects for the past 10 to 15 years. It is a methodology for proactively managing the flow of project work from inception to delivery. Kanban (看板) is the Japanese word for "signboard," in our case, a task board of project work.

Project teams find that visualizing how their workflows provide organization, context, and transparency. In the beginning, it was primarily a DevOps (software) tool; many other types of projects find that it fits their ways of working as well. Many management methods flow from manufacturing, and Kanban did too. Kanban was initially created in the 1940s by Taiichi Ohno as a part of lean manufacturing. Lean and other Six Sigma concepts will be discussed in detail later in the book.

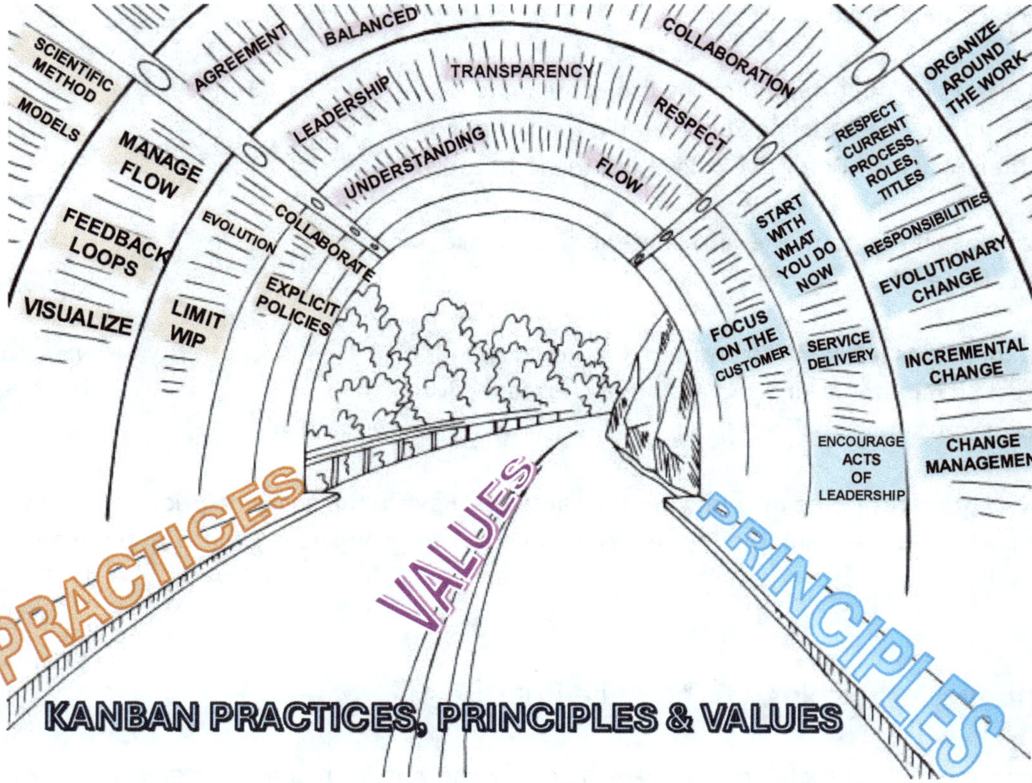

Figure 62. Kanban Practices, Principles, and Values

Practices: (1) Visualize Work, (2) Limit Work in Progress, (3) Manage Flow, (4) Make Process Policies Explicit, (5) Implement Feedback Loops, (6) Improve Collaboratively, Evolve Experimentally

Principles: (1) Start With What You Do Now, (2) Agree to Pursue Incremental, Evolutionary Change, (3) Encourage Acts of Leadership at All Levels, (4) Focus on Customers' Needs and Expectations, (5) Manage the Work, (6) Regularly Review the Network of Services

Values: (1) Understanding, (2) Agreement (3) Respect, (4) Leadership, (5) Self-Organization, (6) Flow, (7) Customer Focus, (8) Transparency, (9) Balance, (10) Collaboration, (11) Resilience

Visualizing the Workflow

An Agile board can range from a low-tech whiteboard with sticky notes to a high-tech project management application that shows the current sprint's user stories and progress. It comprises columns representing the stages of work, and sticky notes, cards, etc., represent the work as it moves through the project management process. Each card represents a task from the backlog assigned to a person or group.

Columns - stages of the team's workflow

Cards - individual units of work

WIP - the maximum number of work items that can be in each workflow stage at any given time.

Swimlanes - horizontal divisions that can be utilized to separate and categorize various activities

Tags - categorizing, arranging, and filtering, and tasks that require attention

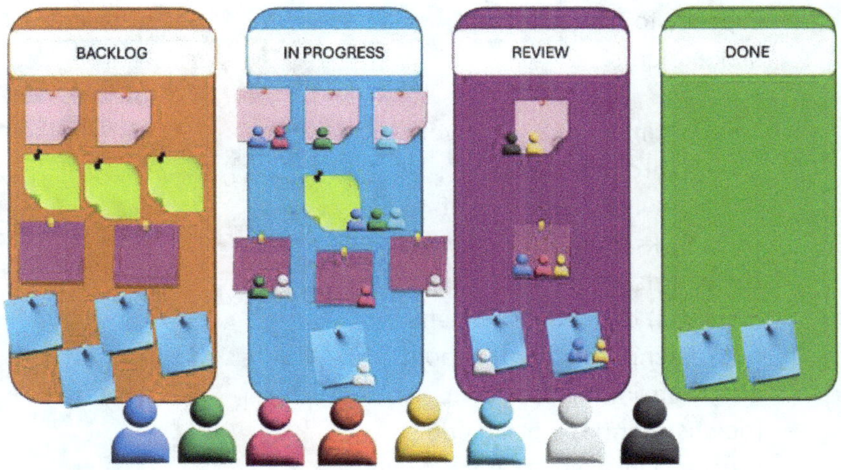

Figure 63. The Kanban Backlog

Each card will include the information needed for the specific project type.

For example, in manufacturing, it may include the part number, product ID, bar code, supplier, etc. For others, it may consist of the requirement's unique ID, the activity's number or name, who's working on it, the estimated time to completion, and any blockers hindering progress.

Figure 64. The Kanban Sticky Note

Pull System Framework - Managing the Flow

Using the pull system helps ensure your team completes the work in front of them before taking on new tasks. The columns visually show that each team member has limited capacity for the team and stakeholders.

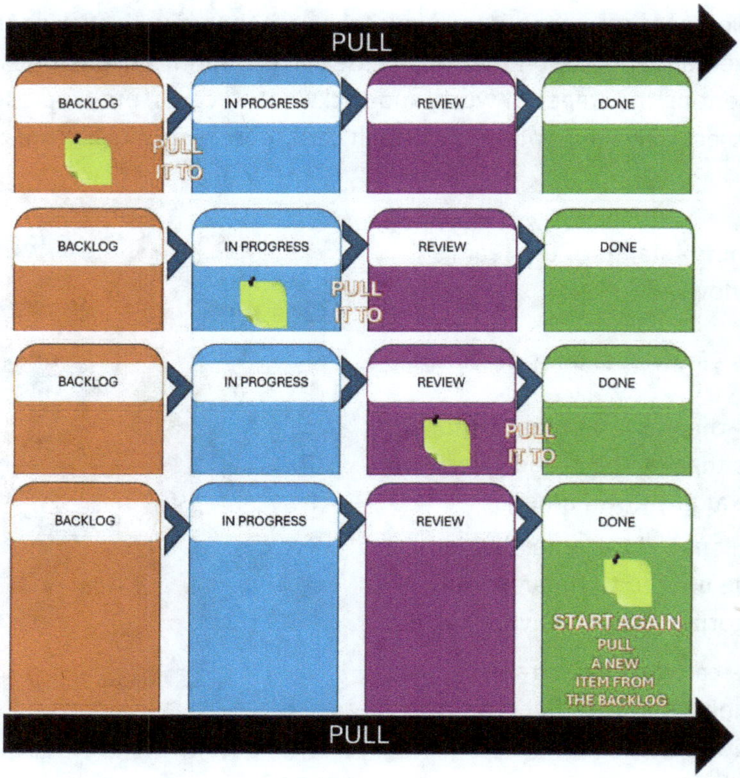

Figure 65. The Kanban Pull System

This continuity of steady work is built through "signaling": only allowing the pulling of fresh tasks into the column on the boards when there's space (demand) to handle them and not replenishing them without a signal from further down (downstream) the production process. Once a work item card moves over to "done," they can pull an item from "to-do" to "doing" and repeat the process.

Pull guidelines set limits on in-progress efforts, and only pulling fresh work with open capacity avoids overfilling any segment. Meaning "signal" in Japanese, these cues use visual communication to put a pull system into practice. Kanban is a framework of pull signals. These signals permit work to be replaced or refilled and are called **Kanbans**.

This Kanban framework uncovers and helps overcome the three main roadblocks that negatively impact the project work: (1) muda or wasteful activities, (2) muri or the overburden of workers, and (3) mura or unevenness.

Muda, Mura, and Muri

Muda is the Japanese word for waste. This is any activity that does not add value to the creation of the product or service for the customer. Using a Kanban board helps pinpoint areas where Muda exists. In project management, it helps identify where the project team's energy can be most useful to the project.

Mura is the Japanese word for unevenness or variation. In viewing the cards on the Kanban board, the project team can easily pinpoint the flow of work and thus inconsistencies in the amount of work in progress (WIP). Being able to see where work is waiting and other factors affecting work completion allows for adjustments to improve the flow of work in each iteration.

Muri is the Japanese word for overburden. This is placing too much strain on the project's resources. It can explain why team members are working overtime to meet targets, why there is variation in the pace of work, or why they are being exerted beyond their capacity. Overburdening the project team could lead to low morale, defects, and downtime.

Using the Kanban board effectively can go a long way toward setting up the project team with streamlined processes. By paying attention to the board, teams can catch these flow problems early. Breaking work into small, achievable chunks reduces lead times and improves efficiency. Optimizing workflow in line with the team's capacity helps eliminate bottlenecks and unexpected issues.

Work in Progress (WiP)

Represents the maximum number of tasks being worked on by an individual or team in the workflow at one time. Together, the team determines the WIP limits for each status or column.

The workflow's owning team identifies WiP limits. Setting WiP limits is a key property in Kanban. Setting WiP limits forces teams to work only on what they can improve, increasing throughput and reducing the amount of work "nearly done" by ensuring they focus only on specifically assigned tasks and not context-switching or multitasking.

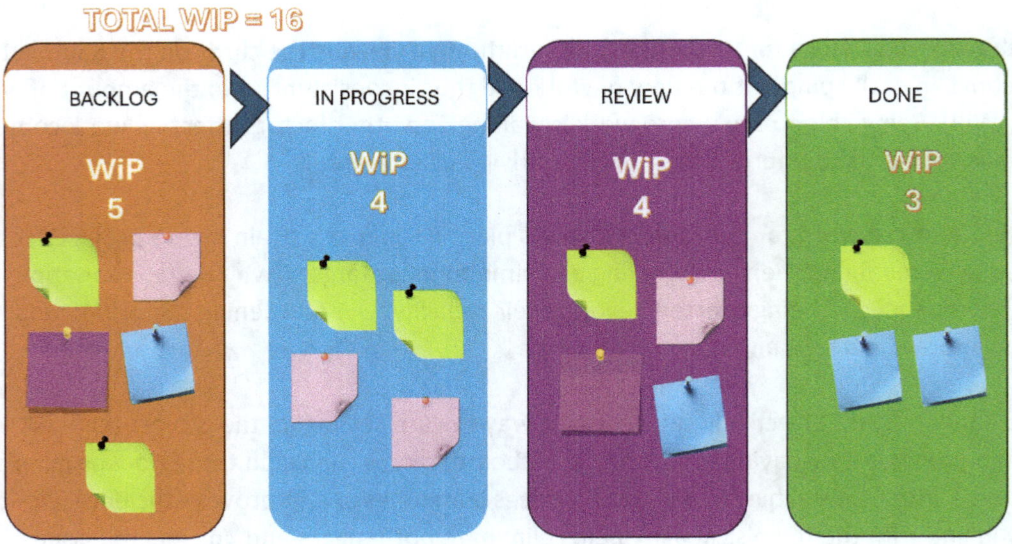

Figure 66. Calculating WiP Limits

Extreme Programming (XP)

Extreme Programming is an agile software development framework that emphasizes engineering practices. It is used in conjunction with other Agile methodologies. XP has been around since the 90s, when Ken Beck, while working on the Comprehensive Compensation (C3) program at Chrysler, aimed to improve the system's performance. To fix the problems with the project, Beck understood that using XP would empower developers to respond to changing requirements, trim unnecessary activities, and reduce time and costs while producing high-quality code. XP is the practice of excellence when confronted with dynamically changing software requirements.

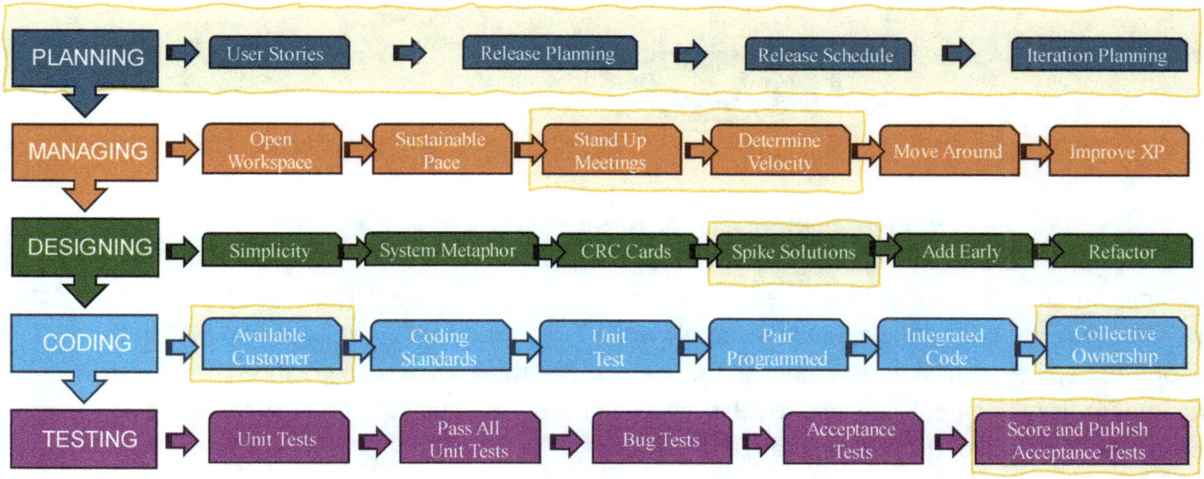

Figure 67. Extreme Programming Phases

Extreme Programmers constantly communicate with the project Team. XP teams are best when they are small, collocated, and spontaneous when appropriate. There is constant communication in the coding and team workspaces. It relies on continuous feedback loops to solve its problems. They get feedback by testing their software starting on day one.

The Project Flow for XP

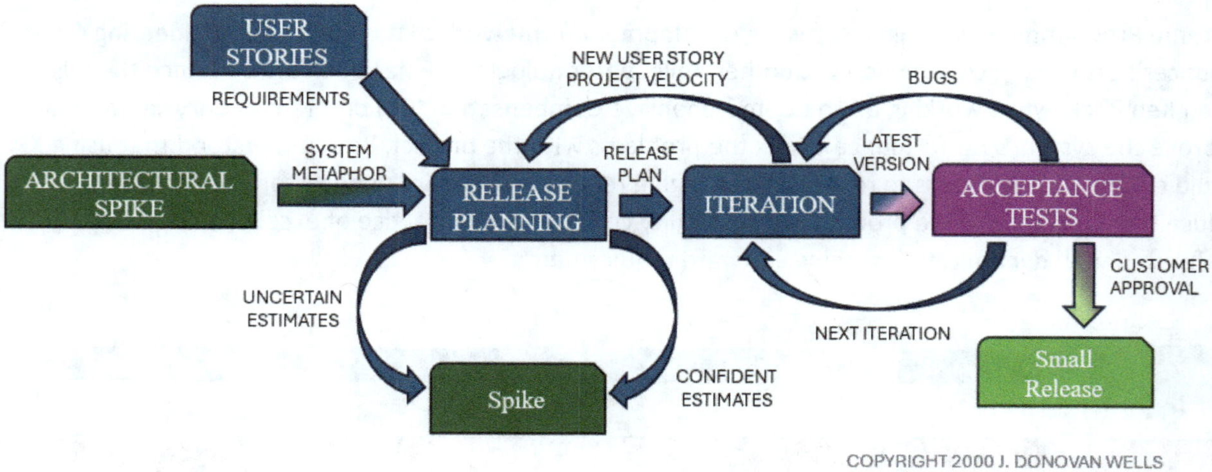

Figure 68. Project Flow for the Extreme Programming Methodology

The XP methodology fits within the core agile process. Developers review user stories with the project team and break them into manageable pieces of work. The participants in release planning and development spikes from the items chosen for the next iteration. They then go about the work of development using elements specific to XP, such as pair programming, refactoring, testing, and acceptance testing, until the code is ready for release.

Some elements are shared among the project team. One is that all work is created through collective effort, meaning everyone contributes and everyone owns the ideas and the results. With **Collective Ownership,** the entire team is responsible for the system's design.

At the beginning of the iteration, the developer will take a user story (requirement) and develop a small technical experiment, building working software to prove or disprove the feasibility of a specific hypothesis called an **Architectural Spike**. This not only allows testing whether the work should be included in the system but also enables developers to give the project manager a more accurate estimate of the project or iteration velocity.

The **iteration velocity** is the agreed-upon amount that will be completed in an iteration. To measure the **project velocity**, all of the estimates from all of the user stories are added up. Once the stories are broken down into tasks and moved from the backlog during iteration planning, the velocity of that task or activity is measured against the velocity the team has indicated they can handle in the iteration. The planned and actual velocities must be equal. Velocity is a measurement used to track an agile project. If the team is asking for more work or is falling behind, the velocity needs to be pulled into alignment for the next iteration.

Developers use **System Metaphors** to explain a system design to the team without resorting to tech talk, showing code or system designs. This is a way to level the playing field for conversations about the work without developer jargon. These metaphors use everyday language, allowing those with no coding experience to contribute to their work.

The project team uses **Class, Responsibilities, and Collaboration (CRC) Cards** as they meet with developers to contribute to the design of the development work. Each CRC Card represents an object. This meeting, called a CRC session, gives the project team a chance to get on paper the purpose (classes), responsibilities, and collaborators. It is at this time that the project team moves through the process, taking note of any problems or elements that could be strengthened.

Figure 69. Class, Responsibilities, and Collaboration (CRC) Cards

XP requires that developers work in pairs when coding. Pair Programming requires two developers to code together. One machine, one keyboard, one mouse, two brains. Although it may seem awkward at first, it is really the best way to code and proof at the same time. This is not a mentor–mentee situation. These are two developers who, outside of the XP framework, would be responsible for their own high-quality code. Someone is always coding, and the other is thinking and watching. Using this team approach to programming builds in higher-quality code at a faster rate.

Unit tests are pieces of code representing specific functionality of a larger system. During an iteration, developers will, of course, be asked to develop functionality for the software. Developers write unit tests before coding to verify that the code they write meets the requirements.

Developers release unit tests into the code repository along with the code they test. Many times, unit tests are not created because they take time away from the precious time within the iteration. Because there is a risk of buggy code that leads to rework, time for unit testing should be built into the velocity.

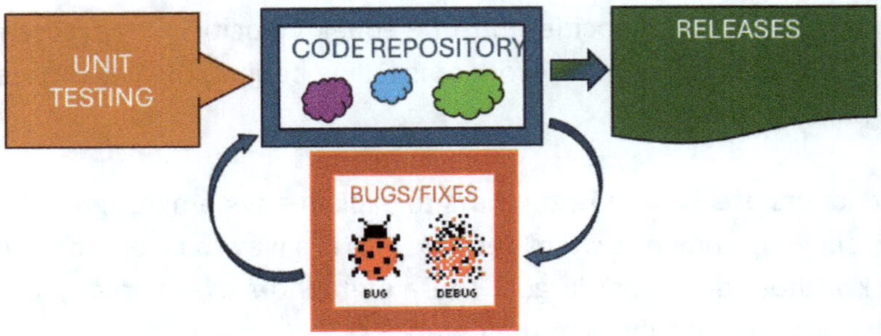

Figure 70. Extreme Programming Test and Release Cycle

Team Roles

- **The Customer** - responsible for making the business decisions for the project.
- **Developers** - responsible for developing the stories for each iteration.
- **Tester –** testing the code for release
- **Manager/The Tracker** keeps track of relevant metrics to track project progress and to identify areas for improvement.
- **The Coach** mentors the project team members on the XP Practices to help the team maintain XP discipline.

Crystal Agile Framework

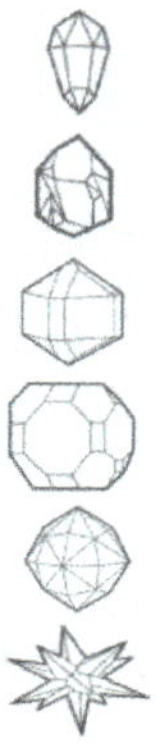

Crystal Agile Methodology focuses on the individuals on the project team and how they interact with others, rather than the project management tools and techniques utilized. This allows for maximum flexibility to capitalize on the uniqueness of each project team.

Every project is unique and always changing, which is why Alistair Cockburn proposed that the project team knew best and should determine how to proceed with the work. As one of the original authors of 'The Agile Manifesto' and 'The Declaration of Interdependence' (highlighted earlier in the chapter), Cockburn developed the Crystal method for IBM in 1991. He broke away from the traditional methods of development strategies and instead developed guidelines for team collaboration and communication. In 1997, he wrote the book "Surviving Object Oriented Projects" about this experience, and a year later developed a family of methodologies and called them "Crystal".

Figure 71. Alistair Cockburn

DECLARATION OF INTERDEPENDENCE

4 We unleash creativity and innovation by recognizing that individuals are the ultimate source of value and creating an environment where they can make a difference.

5 We boost performance through group accountability for results and shared responsibility for team effectiveness.

AGILE MANIFESTO

Individuals and interactions over processes and tools
Working software over comprehensive documentation
Customer collaboration over contract negotiation
Responding to change over following a plan

Teams can find ways on their own to improve and optimize their workflows – tailor the project to make it work. As long as the team kept their eyes on some key principles:

- Frequently delivers high-quality working software
- Communicates with team members constantly
- Continuously improve project communication and processes of engagement and getting the work done through reflection and adaptation
- Keeping the bureaucracy and documentation to a minimum

Figure 72. Seven Properties of Crystal Clear

Frequent delivery: Regular releases of working software to gather feedback and adapt quickly

Reflective improvement: Continuous evaluation and adjustment of processes

Osmotic communication: Close, face-to-face interaction among team members

Personal safety: Creating an environment where team members feel safe to share ideas and concerns

Focus: Providing uninterrupted time for team members to concentrate on their work

Easy access to expert users: Ensuring regular interaction with end-users or domain experts

Technical environment: Providing the necessary tools and infrastructure for efficient development

The Crystal Team Color Methodology - the number of people in the project, which is indicated by different colors.

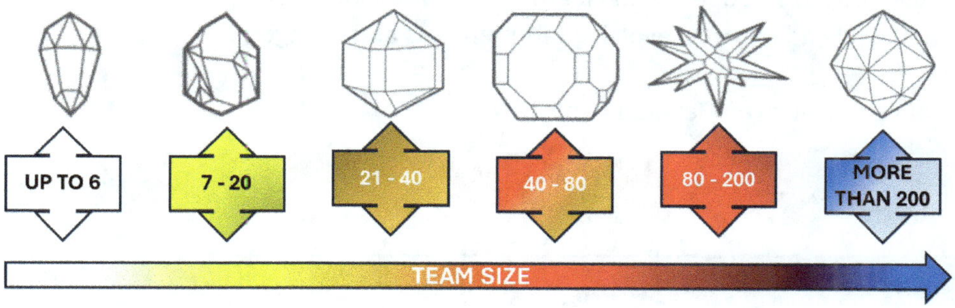

Figure 73. Team Sizes of Crystal Clear

Crystal Diamond and Crystal Sapphire: Both are methods used for highly critical, large-scale projects. These vertical factors are used in conjunction with team size. Their team and strategies are determined based on the project's criticality.

This adaptive methodology empowered team members to collaborate openly and often to find the best ways to get the project work done. Using the highly adaptive Crystal method is not without its drawbacks. With teams doing what they want, how they want, sponsors, executives, and even management have less visibility into how the work is being done and how to measure it from project to project.

Feature-Driven Development (FDD) Methodology

The Feature-Driven Development (FDD) Methodology is best suited for complex, long-term projects. FDD offers project teams flexibility and scalability by dividing feature sets into manageable parts through iterative work and releases. The project workflow revolves around development and release cycles of feature iterations. The main objective of the FDD project's iterations is to deliver a well-developed, fully tested, and operational feature. FDD differs from SCRUM in that FDD emphasizes documentation while adapting to evolving requirements and changes.

Five Phases of Feature-Driven Development

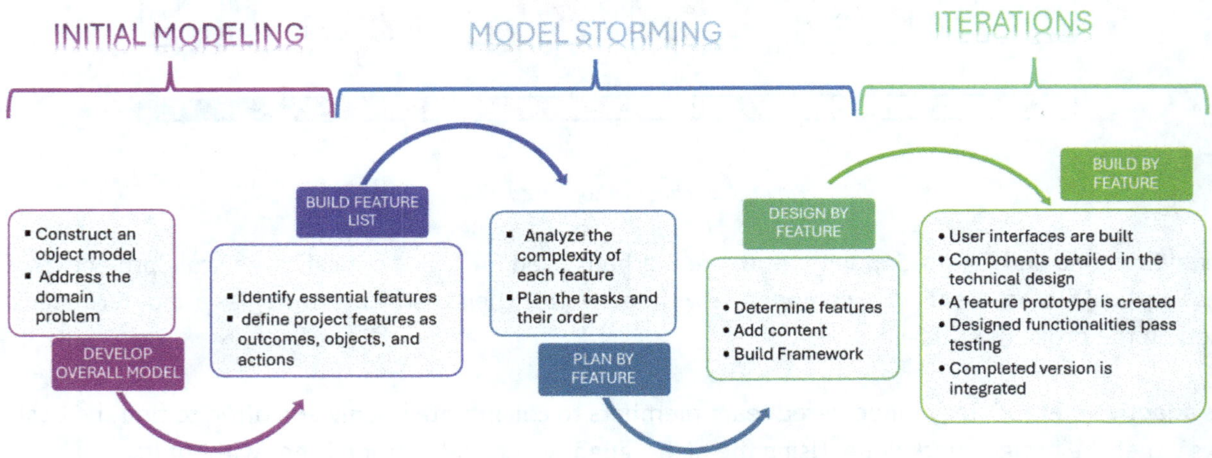

Figure 74. Five Phases of Feature-Driven Development

Initial Modeling

Developing an Overall Model: The project team constructs an object model to address the domain problem. The FDD team (developers, domain experts, and a chief programmer) works collaboratively through each iteration.

Model Storming

Building a Features List: This process is very similar to creating a SCRUM product backlog. The team identifies essential features and defines project features as outcomes, objects, and actions.

Planning by Feature: The project team organizes and prioritizes the implementation of features, assigning them to programmers and developers.

1. Analyze the complexity of each feature
2. Further evaluation and grouping of the features using:
    a. dependencies
    b. obstacles and potential risks, team and individual workload
3. Plan tasks for each of the related features
4. Determine the order in which each feature will be implemented
5. Assigned team members to each feature set
    a. . . . .. . responsible for the conceptual principles of that class
    b. Identify class owners, individual developers who are assigned to classes

Designing by Feature (DFB): Adding content and inspection by the client

1. A chief programmer will determine the feature that will be designed and built. Specifically, they will:
    a. determine the class owners
    b. feature teams involved
    c. defining the feature priorities
    d. Everyone else will work on the framework collaboratively to analyze and design solutions for each feature

Building by Feature (BBF): Often the longest step in the FDD process

1. The approaches and components for the feature design are implemented. User interfaces are built using Components detailed in the technical design. A feature prototype is created
2. Designed functionalities pass testing, the completed version is integrated into the project's main codebase and deployed for client use.

Benefits of Feature-Driven Development

- Provides scalability
- Provides predictability by breaking the project into manageable features and quick delivery
- Ensures code quality and integrity
- Provides flexibility

Dynamic Systems Development Method (DSDM)

DSDM is an Agile method that focuses on the entire project lifecycle, created in January 1994 (the first version was completed in January 1995) by the DSDM Consortium (a non-profit) in the UK. It was built on the Rapid Application Development (RAD) approach to software development. It is an iterative and incremental approach that emphasizes continuous communication and collaboration between the customer and the client.

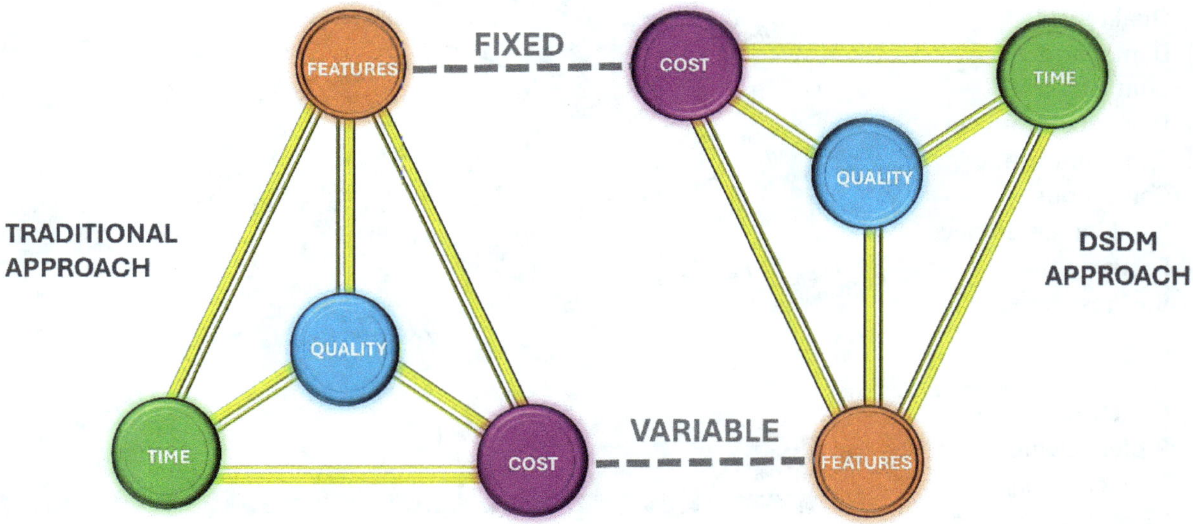

Figure 75. Traditional Versus Variable Project Management Approaches

DSDM deals with projects rather than just the development and delivery of a software product. It focuses on the formula: 80% system deployment in 20% time.

THE PRINCIPLES, DEVELOPMENT PROCESS, AND ROLES OF DSDM

Principles:

(1) Cooperate and Collaborate
(2) Never Compromise Quality
(3) Demonstrate Control
(4) Develop Iteratively
(5) Communicate Continuously
(6) Build Incrementally
(7) Focus on the Business Need

Roles:

- Directors
- Project Owners
- Project Managers
- Directors
- Project Owners
- Developers
- Testers

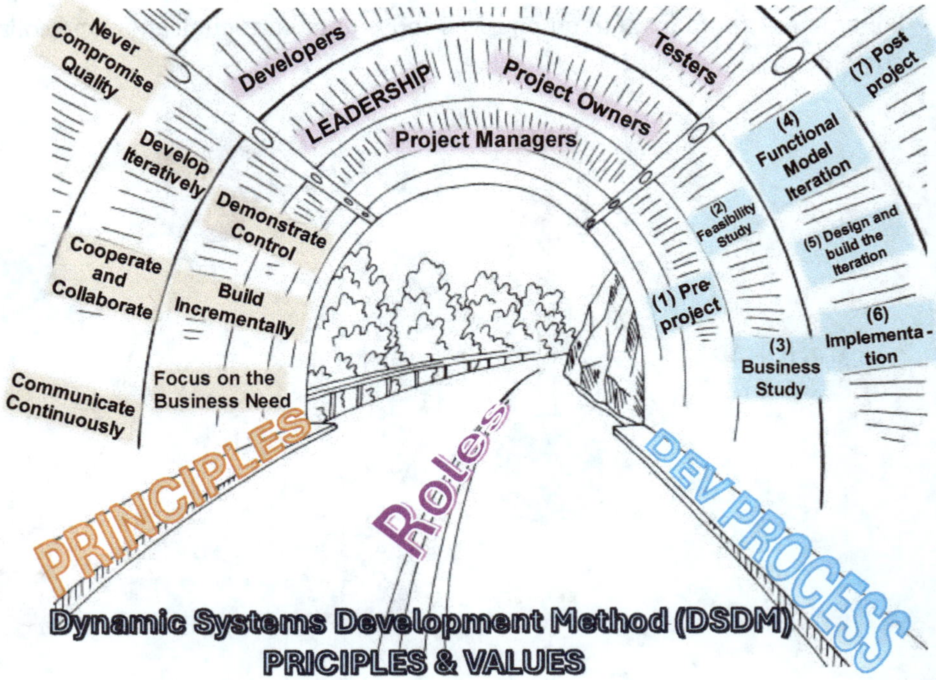

Figure 76. Dynamic Development Method (DSDM) Principles and Values

Development Process:

(1) Pre-project
(2) Feasibility Study
(3) Business Study
(4) Functional Model Iteration
(5) Design and build the Iteration
(6) Implementation
(7) Post-project

The 7 Phases of DSDM

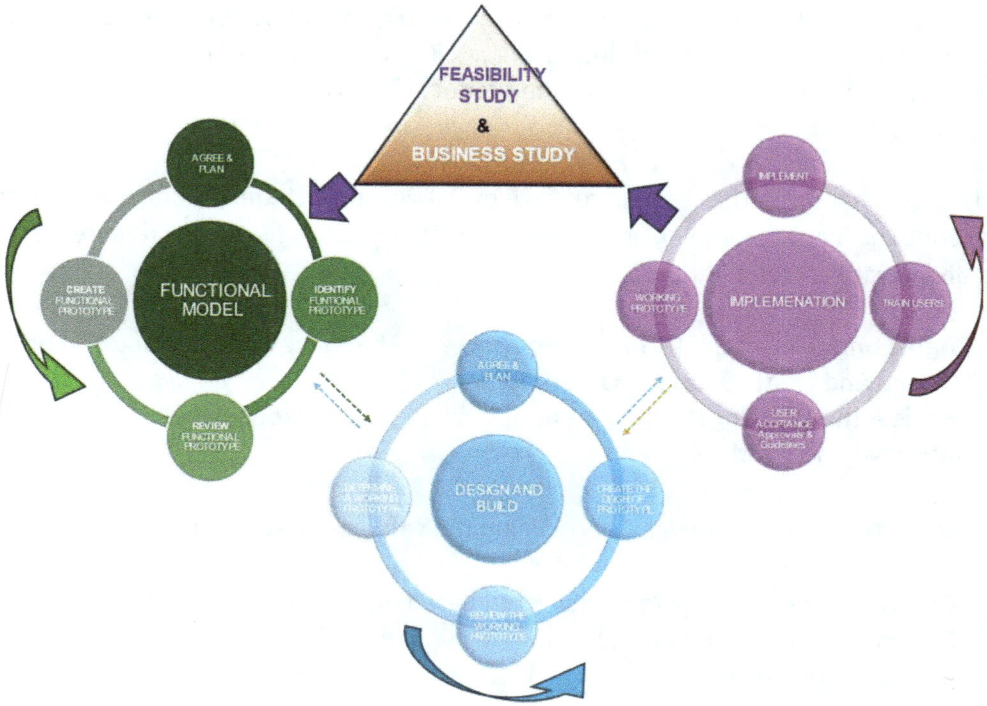

Figure 77. The Seven Phases of DSDM

Pre-project Phase

The team becomes aware of the project's objectives, conceptualizes the work, and determines how and when to start the project.

1. **Feasibility Study** - Feasibility studies help answer the essential question, "Should we proceed with the proposed idea?".
   Feasibility studies help determine whether the company possesses the required resources or technologies, and whether the proposal offers a reasonable return vs. risk from the investment. See Feasibility Study in the Initiation Phase in the Project Management section of this book.

2. **Business Study** *(Business Case)* - The goal of the business case is to determine whether the product or service is really needed, the best way to go about achieving the goal, and how much the endeavor will cost in dollars and resources. The business case helps leaders determine whether the organization can deliver the product or service.
   See Business Case in the Initiation Phase in the Project Management section of this book.

Functional Model Iteration - This is the core stage of DSDM, in which the product is built incrementally, ensuring continuous feedback, tuning, and adaptation. The system's functional requirements are developed and iteratively refined.

1. **Agree and plan all the technical requirements that have been** decided and prioritized.
2. **Design and create** a functional prototype.
3. **Review the Working Prototype** - progressive feedback from users.
4. **Approve and Build.**

Design and build the Iteration - Developers develop the software based on the prototype.

1. **Determine** functionality to be delivered based on the agreed-upon priority.
2. **Design** the prioritized functionality.
3. **Code** the functionality.
4. **Deploy** the functionality

Implementation - The product as a whole will move through the process to deployment, operations, and maintenance (O&M).

1. Assemble a Working Prototype
2. User Acceptance Approvals and Guidelines - all the approvals and guidelines related to the project.
3. Train Users - train users on the product, required configuration, and use.
4. Implement Functionality - Deploy product into operations and maintenance.

Tools and Techniques:

Timeboxing - allocating a specific amount of time to a particular task and then focusing solely on that task within the given time frame.
The concept of timeboxing dates back to the 1980s. Introduced by author James Martin, it was first used in software development to manage the complexities of the development process.

Facilitated Workshops – Meetings that bring people together from several business areas to allow for streamlined knowledge sharing opportunities.
Gives stakeholders a greater sense of involvement for the participants and their ownership of the outcome—a catalyst for enhanced communication and much-improved decision-making.

Iterative Development - approaches the project using feedback loops. This approach allows the project team to succeed or fail fast and learn fast to improve the next iteration.
An incremental life cycle uses a set time to complete testable work while moving towards larger and, of course, the final deliverable.

Modeling & Prototyping Techniques - a basic version of a software or hardware product, often built to test a concept or process.
The word prototype comes from the Latin words proto, meaning original, and typus, meaning form or model.

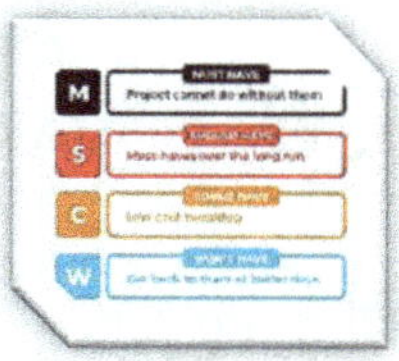

MoSCow Prioritization

Must-Have: The requirements that are fundamental and must conform to the solution.
Should Have: The things that are important for the business solution.
Could Have: The requirements that are important but can more easily be left out for a while.
Won't Have: The requirements that can wait and be included in later development.

Adaptive Project Framework (APF)

The focus of APF is adapting to changing requirements, environments, and client and stakeholder needs. This is a unique project methodology based on systematic client control over project details.

A project team should use APF when they need to be responsive and adaptive to change, be innovative and willing to experiment, and encourage failure to spur iterative improvements.

There are five key steps or phases within the APF. Although it is defined as an iterative or cyclical approach

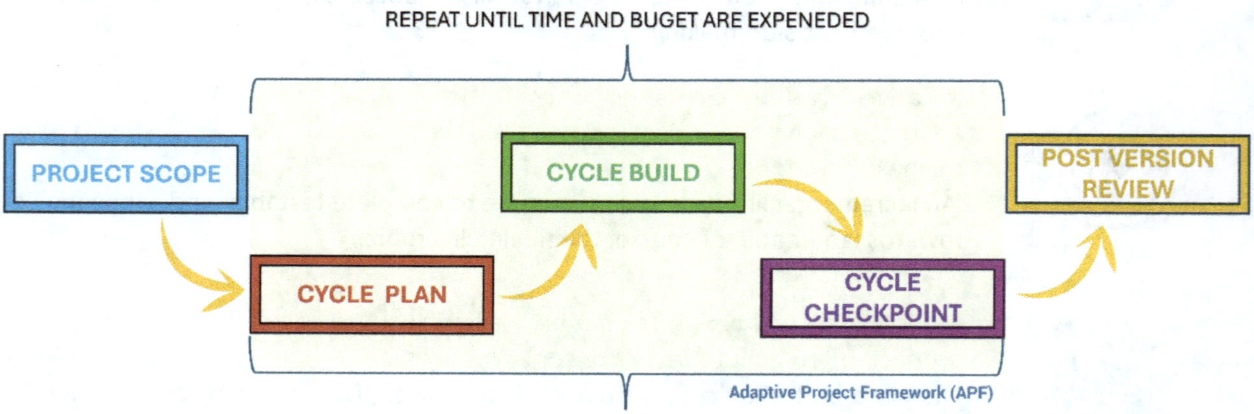

Figure 78. Cycle of the Adaptive Project Framework (APF)

Benefits to APF

- Client-focused
- Client-driven
- Change-focused
- Prioritization of requirements
- Continuous feedback

Disadvantages to APF

- Ambiguity in process
- Cycles (Iterations) are not flexible; change requests need to wait
- Scope creep

Phase 1
Project scope.

- Conditions of Satisfaction (CoS).
- Project overview Statement (PoS).
- Requirement prioritisation
- Work Breakdown Structure (WBS).
- Scope triangle prioritisation.

Phase 2
Cycle Schedule.

- Tasks within the WBS need to be defined
- Task dependencies outlined
- Tasks are grouped and assigned to project team members
- Effective work schedule is created

Phase 3
Cycle build

- Undertaking agreed upon & scheduled work
- Monitoring & controlling progress and adjusting as required
- Completing the cycle at the scheduled date
- Reallocating pending tasks
- Documenting feedback & improvements
- Tracking problems & implementing solutions.

Phase 4
Client checkpoint.

- Feedback is provided by stakeholders around what was delivered in the previous cycle build.
- liaise with the clients and stakeholders to adjust the upcoming schedule or deliverables as needed.
- Any changes are documented and consideration is given to how quality will be assessed.

Phase 5
Final report.

- A collaborative effort between the project team, stakeholders, and client.
- All of thesuccesses & failures are documented, improvements are considered & experiences are shared.
- The final report should support future projects.

Figure 79. 5 key steps or phases within the Adaptive Project Framework (APF)

CHAPTER FOUR: SIX SIGMA

Project Management using Data and Analysis

In this chapter, you will learn

- What is Lean Six Sigma?
- Lean Six Sigma Tools and Techniques
- Six Sigma and the Organization
- The Six Sigma List

WHAT IS LEAN SIX SIGMA?

Six Sigma refers to the practice of delivering products and services that perform at high standards. It is the pursuit of perfection that results in delays, unpredictable, undesirable outcomes, and limits. In projects, this is done by identifying opportunities for improvement in the design stages of your project iterations. Lean is the pursuit of improvement towards excellence in products, services, processes, and people. In other words, removing any non-value adding (NVA) activities. Lean Six Sigma follows the equation:

Figure 80. Lean 6 Sigma Equation

Applying lean and six sigma tools in your everyday project management work involves improving quality by identifying and removing the causes of defects and minimizing variability. A continuous improvement mindset is the foundation of why projects exist. Project Managers are in the improvement business. With the move to agile project management, improving processes as the project progresses.

We use the Greek letter 'Sigma,' a Greek letter and mathematical term, to denote standard deviation. It is a standard statistical unit used to measure and describe the distribution of any process about its mean. Plainly – **How good you are!** The 68-95-99.7 rule, also known as the empirical rule, is used to remember the percentage of values that lie within a band around the mean in a normal distribution, with widths of one, two, and three standard deviations, as we move toward perfection.

Table 9. The Empirical Rule

1σ=68.26%		2σ=95.46%	
3σ=99.73%	4σ=99.9937	5σ=99.9999943%	6σ=99.9999996%

The Belts

Six Sigma certifications are identified by colored belts, from least experienced to most experienced.

White Belt 	☐ Has a basic understanding of Six Sigma concepts and terminology ☐ Assist with change management ☐ Participate in local problem-solving teams that support larger projects
Yellow Belt 	☐ Has a deeper understanding of Six Sigma principles ☐ Assist Green and Black Belts in data collection and analysis ☐ Assist project leaders in implementing process changes ☐ Lead smaller projects or initiatives under the guidance of higher-level Belts.
Green Belt 	☐ Has a solid understanding of Six Sigma methodologies and tools ☐ Leads smaller projects ☐ Serves as a team member on larger projects led by Black Belts. Completed full course training on the methodology and can participate in projects, but won't lead them ☐ They lead teams and work on Six Sigma projects on a part-time basis

Black Belt 	☐ Completed extensive training in Six Sigma methodology to lead complex projects and organizational change ☐ Mentors Green and Yellow Belts ☐ Manages multiple projects across different departments ☐ Key to driving significant changes within an organization
Master Black Belt 	☐ The highest level of Six Sigma certification ☐ Has extensive experience in Six Sigma ☐ Trains and mentors Black Belts and Green Belts ☐ Oversee the implementation of Six Sigma methodologies across the enterprise ☐ Provide expert guidance on complex projects
Champions 	☐ The organization's strategic and tactical business leaders. ☐ They approve Six Sigma project charters, review project progress, and ensure the success of Six Sigma projects in their business units.

The History of Lean and Six Sigma

We can trace Six Sigma, as a measurement standard for product variation, back to 1910, when Henry Ford implemented lean strategies in the manufacturing of cars. The 1920s, when Walter Shewhart showed that three sigma from the mean is the point where a process requires correction. And the 1930s with Toyota. The term Six Sigma was first coined by American Motorola Engineer Bill Smith in 1986, who is known as the father of Six Sigma.

Table 10. The Founding Fathers of Quality and Their Tools

The Founding Fathers of Quality	TOOLS
 **Walter A Shewhart** **Father of Statistical Quality Control**	Used statistics to make material improvements in processes and reduce variation to improve quality. Shewhart was ASQ's first honorary associate, and he efficaciously brought together the principles of statistics, economics, and engineering. Special variation vs Common cause variation. Invented Plan-Do-Study-Act as a design approach. Invented control charts, Theory about statistical control methods
 **Joseph Juran** **Architect of Quality - Quality Trilogy**	"It is most important that top management be quality-minded. In the absence of sincere manifestation of interest at the top, little will happen below." Quality cost measurement and the Managing for Quality theory Pareto analysis, Quality Planning, Quality Control, and Quality Improvements

 W. Edwards Deming **7 Deadly diseases of management: Improving the system**	Maintained that senior management involvement was critical to a quality movement. Chain Reaction of Quality: "Improve Quality, Decrease Costs, Improve Productivity, Capture the market with better Quality and price, Stay in business, and Provide Jobs" Plan-Do-Study-Act cycle into widespread usage.
 Jaoru Ishikawa **Father of Japanese Quality**	Played a key role in the development of a specifically Japanese quality strategy. Invented CWQC – Company Wide Quality Control. Sponsored the concept of "next operation (process step) as the client" to avoid workplace politics. Fishbone diagram (4M/5M or cause and effect diagram) and the TQM– Fiegenbaum and Ishikawa (1980s)
 Genichi Taguchi **Robust Design & Loss Function**	The Taguchi robustness approach says that various factors control processes or products to get the desired response. Quality is related to the financial loss to society caused by a product during its life cycle. Introduce quality in the conceptual phase, bring it through the design phase, and eventually into manufacturing operations. Taguchi Loss Function and the Taguchi Robust Design

 **Philip B. Crosby** **zero defects & defining quality as conformance to requirements**	14 Step approach to Quality Improvements and the 4 Absolutes of Quality Management: Quality is conformance to requirements; quality comes from prevention; quality performance standards are zero defects; quality measurement is the price of non-conformance; and quality costs are created.
 **Armand V. Feigenbaum** **Established the concept of Total Quality Control & Management (TQM)**	Presented with the National Medal of Technology and Innovation by President Bush. The National Medal is the highest honor for technological achievement bestowed on America's leading innovators. Known for his concept of the "hidden plant", which states that in every factory, a proportion 9up to 40% of the capacity is wasted through not getting it right the first time.
 **Bill Smith** **Father of Six Sigma - Motorola**	"If you want to improve something, involve the people who are doing the job." First introduced the term Six Sigma. In 1987, he joined Motorola as VP & Sr. QA manager for the 'Land Mobile'. Convinced Motorola CEO, Robert W Galvin, to adopt Six Sigma.

<table>
<tr><td></td><td rowspan="2">Six Sigma: The Breakthrough Management Strategy Revolutionizing the World's Top Corporations - a bestseller
Assisted in developing MAIC that evolved into DMAIC.

2002 lifetime Engineering Excellence Award from Arizona State University & the "Who's Who" Registry of Global Business Leaders in 1993.</td></tr>
<tr><td>Mikel Harry
Main Architect of Six Sigma</td></tr>
</table>

THE SIX SIGMA PROJECT LIFECYCLE: DMAIC

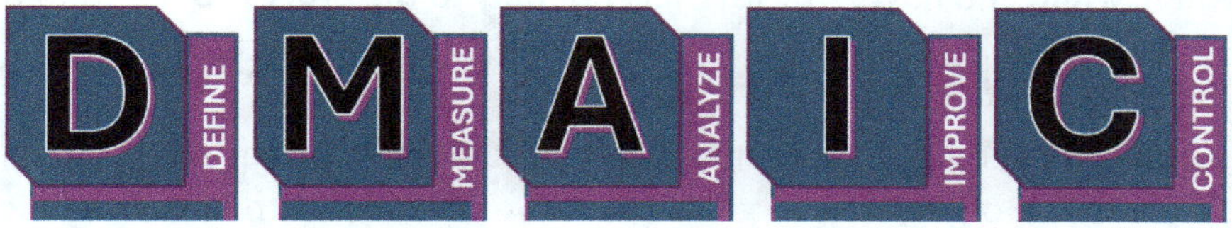

Figure 81. The DMAIC Model

The 5 phases include: defining the problem, analyzing the root causes, improving the process or product, and controlling the process or outcomes. The Six Sigma methodology follows a structured data-driven approach known as DMAIC (Define, Measure, Analyze, Improve, Control). These can easily be extended to project iterations. In agile project management, improvements are built into the design phases of each iteration. By adding data and analysis, the project team can ensure they are building elements into the product that add value.

The Define Phase

The Define Phase is based on understanding the problem under investigation. Basically, getting a complete understanding of who needs this product and why. It is here; the project team defines the problem, goal, requirements, and project scope. They create a project charter, map the processes, and identify issues, key metrics, and deliverables. May tools and techniques will be provided to elicit answers to these questions and map their initiation.

Let's look at some key factors that need to be addressed in the define phase:

What is the goal or outcome we wish to achieve? Are we looking to reduce cost, time, or resources? Are we looking for more efficient or effective ways of working? Have we compared ourselves to industry standards and realized we need to do better or keep up? All of these are valid reasons to undertake a Six Sigma project. Now is the time to determine what fits your specific undertaking. This can be done by first answering some high-level key questions—where, when, what, and how — by listening not only to the process but also to the customers.

Voice of the Customer (VoC): The needs and requirements of the customers for the output under investigation. The goal is to fulfill the organization's goals and move towards customer satisfaction. It is essential to identify the customers and their needs and requirements. The communication plan is also important for listening to the voice of the customer throughout the project, using proactive rather than reactive methods – don't wait for negative feedback! Metrics on satisfaction constructs are harvested through listening to the voice of the customer through surveys, feedback forms, focus groups, and interviews. Some of these metrics include friendliness, responsiveness, timeliness, competency, and consistency.

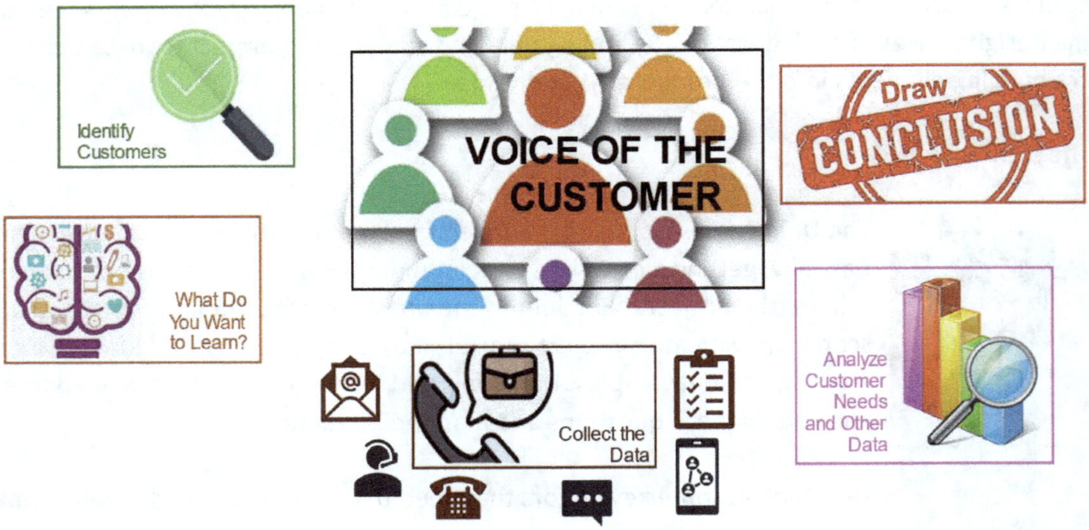

Figure 82. Steps in Understanding the Voice of the Customer (VoC)

All customers and stakeholders should be identified from the outset of the project, as they are the recipients of the effort. You absolutely need their feedback to collect requirements and ensure customer satisfaction with the product. You will use continuous feedback (critical to quality measures) when choosing and prioritizing the product's features and sign off on them when they are developed and tested.

Creating a communication plan for stakeholders is important documentation in every flavor of project management, and with Six Sigma, it is a driving force.

The Problem Statement is a key section of a project charter, regardless of whether it is a traditional, agile, or Six Sigma project.

- ☐ Where are we having problems?
- ☐ When are these problems occurring?
- ☐ What systems, resources, etc., are contributing to these problems?
- ☐ How do we know—have there been complaints, or was it measured in some way?
- ☐ How much is the problem costing us – or better yet, how much can we save by improving the problem?

Once the right questions are asked, we go about the business of doing the work to get these questions concretely answered with data. The strength of Six Sigma is that project decisions are based on quantitative measures in the measure phase. Even though customer opinions are significant, it is now time to quantify them using qualitative data. That's the strength of Six Sigma.

The Six Sigma Project Charter

One of the main deliverables is the project charter that serves as a roadmap for the project. It ensures that team members and stakeholders understand the project's goal and are aligned with it. It also serves as the contract between the project manager, the Six Sigma Belt, and the Sponsor as to what is to be accomplished by the initiative. Similar to the project management charter, it defines the iron triangle of scope, quality, and budget.

Process Improvement Initiative Project Charter			
Project Title:			
Agency:		Division:	
Business Case:			
Opportunity for Improvement:			
Goal Statement:			

Project Scope		
In Scope/ Out Scope:	IN-SCOPE	OUT OF SCOPE

Project Benefits				
Benefits Category	Benefit Description	Measurements		
		Metric	Current State	Target
Cost Savings				
Customer Satisfaction				
Time				
Quality Improvement				

Project Risks			
Risk (Future)	Issues (Current)	Constraints	

Project Schedule					
Project Key Milestones	Define	Measure	Analyze	Improve	Control
Target Start Date:					
Target Completion Date:					

Project Team Members			
Team Members	Name	Agency / Team	Title

Project Approvals			
Resource	Name	Signature	Date
Process Sponsor			
Process Owner			
Process Improvement Lead			

Figure 83 Six Sigma Project Charter

A good project charter defines the following in clear detail:

- **Business case:** Justifies the need for the project
- **Problem statement:** Defines the issue to be addressed
- **Goal statement:** Outlines SMART objectives
- **Project scope:** Project boundaries and limitations
- **Timeline and milestones:** A high-level project schedule
- **Project team:** Team members, their roles, and responsibilities

Six sigma, though similar to project management in many ways, has differences:

- **Data-driven approach:** Emphasizes quantifiable data and metrics
- **Process focus:** Specifically focuses on process improvement
- **DMAIC methodology:** Incorporates the **D**efine, **M**easure, **A**nalyze, **I**mprove, and **C**ontrol (DMAIC) framework
- **Statistics:** Emphasis on statistical analysis and data-driven decisions
- **Continuous improvement:** Focuses on cycles of continuous improvement

The Measure Phase

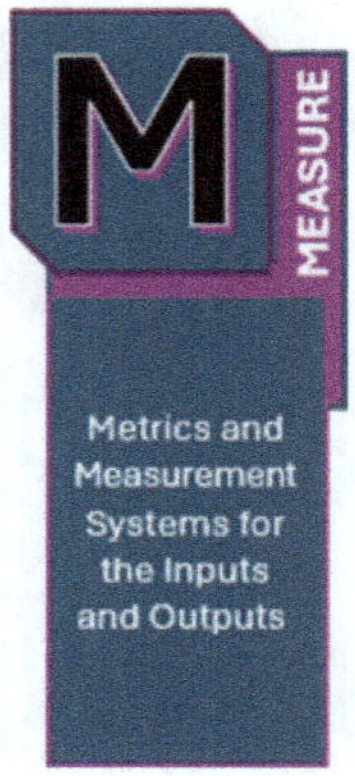

The measure phase examines the current process or product. Using what you learn, a baseline of what is in front of you will lay the foundation for the improvement work ahead. This step is imperative and one of the main differentiators from other project methodologies. Without data and measurements from the current state, anything you build going forward will be built on qualitative analysis and personal judgment, and that is NOT Six Sigma.

The first step is to map the current process using the mapping tools best suited for the processes under examination. This is done by walking through the process, identifying and illustrating all inputs, processing steps, and outputs. There are four views under consideration when mapping a process.

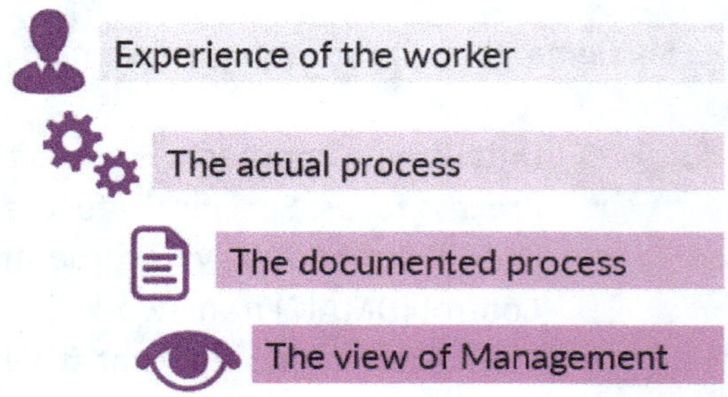

84. The DMAIC - Measure Phase Activities

Data is the backbone, and without it, you cannot analyze the process or make any concrete determination on its value. The data from the processes mapped in the define phase will be used as the baseline for all upcoming activities. In review, the process maps identified data points.

You now know what needs to be measured, who, and what part of the process to harvest the data from. This is important because you are requesting the data you need for your future work. Who do you call when you need data from a particular part of the process? What types and forms of data will you receive, and how often can you request them? The required data will be both qualitative (good/bad, pass/fail) and quantitative (counts, percentages, averages), depending on the part of the process from which it comes. Both are useful

To determine what type of data you need, whether it is helpful, and how it will be used, you will need to create a data collection plan. This plan answers the questions:

- What types of data do you need?
- How will the data be collected, and from whom?
- How much data should be collected, and how will you receive it?

The Analyze Phase

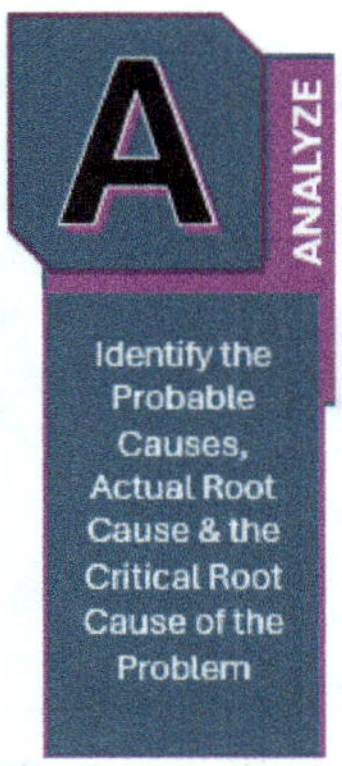

The goal of the third phase of DMAIC is to analyze the data you gathered in the Measure Phase and make sense of it. By making sense of the data presented in the measure phase, the project team has something concrete to look at and is less likely to rush to conclusions about what they 'feel' is wrong and to proceed based on those sometimes unsubstantiated conclusions.

Using definitive data allows for the development of a clear picture of the process under examination and how factors interact, revealing any underlying trends or patterns that can help design solutions to improve the procedure or identify root causes of defects or inefficiencies.

Using tools and techniques like:

- Trend Analysis
- Benchmarking
- Histogram
- Scatterplot
- Cause-effect Analysis
- Survey Method

Shows the project team a few things: (1) the cause of the problem, (2) whether or not to continue with the improvement effort, (2) what kind of improvements to make, and (3) which are the most urgent problems and which ones should be addressed first.

The Improve Phase

The Improve phase focuses on identifying and prioritizing solutions for the problems identified in the first three phases of DMAIC. Solutions to improve a product, service, or process include eliminating wasteful steps, reducing variation, or preventing errors.

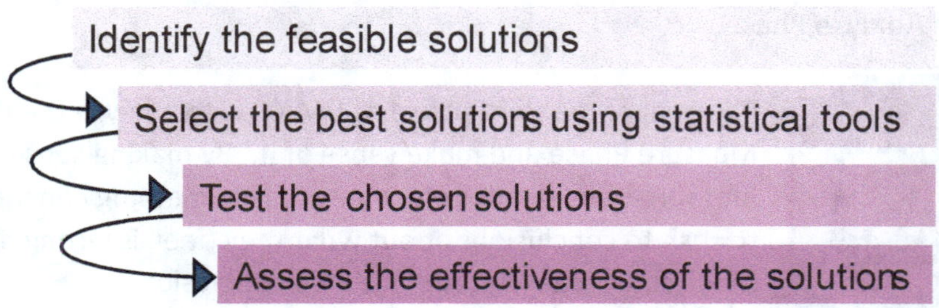

Figure 85. The DMAIC - Improve Process

Potential solutions are evaluated based on cost, resource availability, and implementation time. Project teams should also give special attention to common mistakes in the Improve Phase, which include ineffective (1) pilot testing, (2) change management, (3) monitoring and controls, and (4) deployment.

The Control Phase

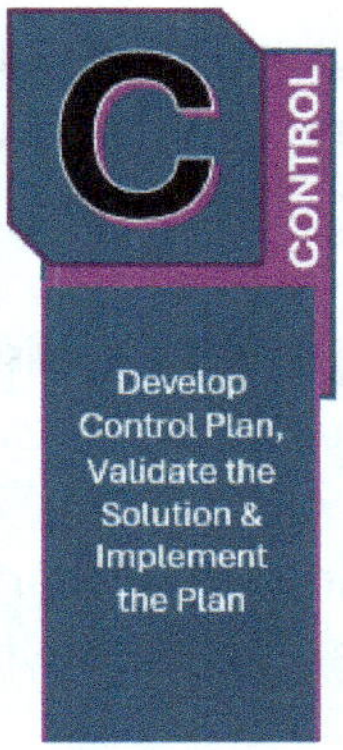

The improved process ensures the new process is implemented and sets guardrails to sustain improvements and, more importantly, prevent them from reverting to pre-improvement levels. Standard Operating Procedures and work instructions are created based on improvements.

Process improvements are controlled through statistical process control methods. Control Charts are the mechanism for process monitoring after improvements are implemented. Acceptable ranges (which are the baseline) for each characteristic improved compared to the new sigma's are carefully and continuously watched for issues, problems, and reversions. Data collected through 24 data points is currently the controlling gold standard. When a process falls outside its acceptable range, the project team should have contingency measures in place for these scenarios.

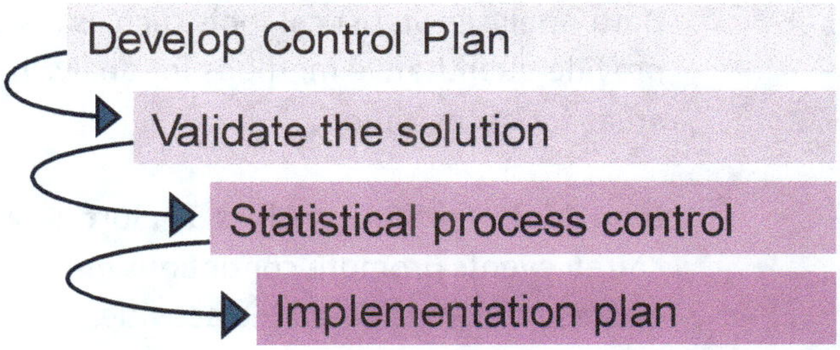

Figure 86. The DMAIC - Control Process

LEAN SIX SIGMA TOOLS AND TECHNIQUES

Lean Six Sigma Tools for Project Management Lean Six Sigma provides a powerful set of tools and techniques that can greatly benefit project management. Some of the key Lean Six Sigma tools used in project management include:

Root Cause Analysis: Techniques such as the 5 Whys, fishbone diagrams, and fault tree analysis enable teams to systematically identify and address the root causes of project issues or defects.

Data Analysis: Statistical tools such as histograms, Pareto charts, scatter plots, and control charts provide quantitative methods for analyzing project data, monitoring performance, and identifying areas for optimization.

Lean Tools: Methods such as 5S (Sort, Straighten, Shine, Standardize, Sustain), Kanban boards, and Kaizen events promote continuous improvement and streamline project workflows by eliminating waste and non-value-added activities.

Project Management Software: Dedicated Lean Six Sigma project management software solutions integrate Six Sigma principles and tools directly into the project management environment, enabling efficient data collection, analysis, and process improvement.

Current State Process Analysis

Defining the current state involves identifying a set of critical elements for the project's success. One of these tools is the SIPOC (Suppliers, Inputs, Processes, Outputs, and Customers) visual, which depicts how a process serves the customer through its inputs and outputs. The next step is actively listening to the voice of the Customer (VOC) through channels such as surveys and focus groups. Once the VOC data is collected, what is done with it is the key to a successful design phase.

Process Mapping: Tools such as process flowcharts, value stream maps, and SIPOC (Suppliers, Inputs, Process, Outputs, Customers) diagrams help visualize and analyze the processes involved in a project. This allows teams to identify waste, inefficiencies, and opportunities for improvement. The elements on the process map should illustrate the who, what, and when of the process or product, with the focus on the what. The process map should be as specific as you need to extract the answers you are looking for. It is best to start with a high-level flow and make it more specific in subsequent steps. For example, once the sequenced high-level steps are mapped, start filling in the details for each process step, including the stakeholders and roles involved, and the decision points. And locations. It illustrated the workflow, information, data, labels, communication, and handoffs of the process.

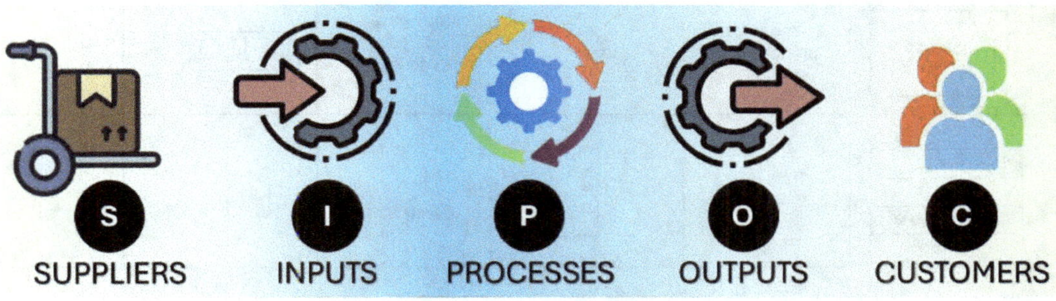

Figure 87. Suppliers, Inputs, Processes, Outputs, and Customers (SIPOC)

Value Stream Mapping

	A	B	C	D	E	F
1	**Symbols**	**Description**	**Symbols**	**Description**	**Symbols**	**Description**
2	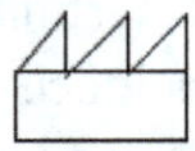	**Customer/ Supplier** Start or end point for material flow		**Kaizen Blitz** Area for Improvement		**External Shipment** Shipments to or from suppliers
3	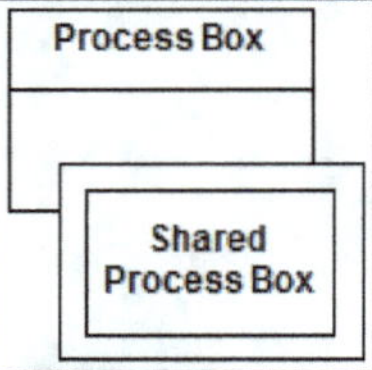	**Process** Machine, operation or department through which material flows	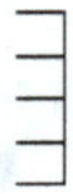	**Supermarket** Small inventory for immediate production	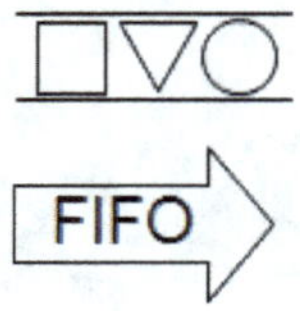	**FIFO** First in, First out lane
4	P/T = 15 L/T = 15 %C&A = 99% Rel. = 95%	**Data Box**	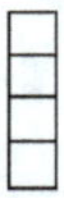	**Buffer** Safety Stock		**In Box** Information Queues

Value stream maps illustrate the parts of the process, so a determination of where the value lies can be made. Mike Rother and John Shook introduced Value Stream Maps as 'material and information flow diagrams' at Toyota. Value stream mapping is an essential part of the define process, where the value to the customer is determined. It pinpoints the value- and non-value-added activities of both internal and external participants.

SIPOC

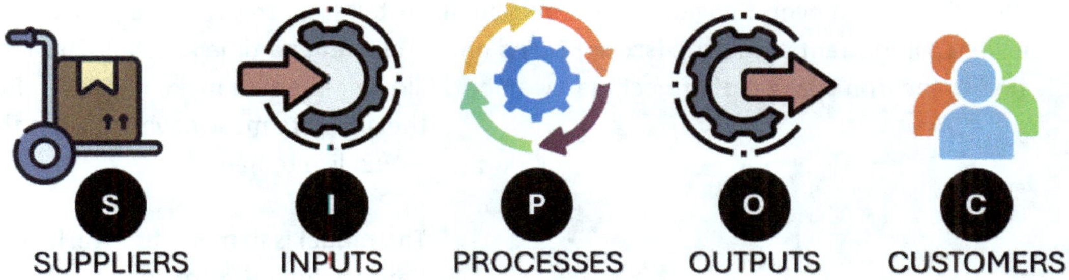

The next best Six Sigma practice is to create a map of the value of the process. SIPOCs (Suppliers, Inputs, Processes, Outputs, and Customers) are connected to the business objectives, which are broken down into their key components. This works by illustrating the inputs to the process, the process itself, and the resulting outputs, which feed back on the variable that requires change to improve the process in the next iteration.

Kano Diagrams

Stakeholders likely want everything on their requirements list. It is up to you to help them prioritize what's important to include (scope) based on the budget and time allotted. This is directly tied to the iron triangle of project management. Allowing them to make decisions, from the absolute must-haves to what they would like to have.

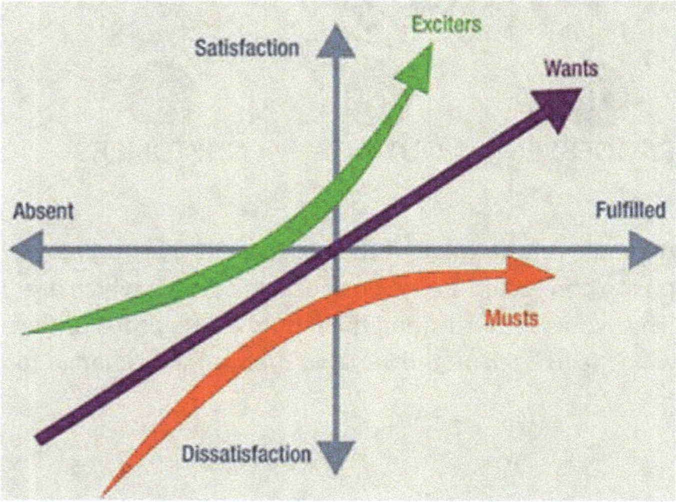

Table 11. Kano Diagram

The model is named after **Noriaki Kano**, a Japanese consultant who first described it in the 1980s in a paper published in the Journal of the Japanese Society for Quality Control.

Must-be qualities – Are the most important requirements and consist of the features that the application or system that are obvious for the application to function.

One-dimensional qualities – Are the features that are not required for the application to function but are required for usability. These features usually make or break user opinions.

Attractive qualities - Are the features that push the application from good to great. They make the application or system user-friendly in ways that users appreciate.

Indifferent qualities – The features that would be included that have no significant effect on user experience, and they won't be missed if they weren't included or removed.

Reverse qualities are actually features that hurt the customer's user experience.

Input-Output (IPO) Analysis Technique

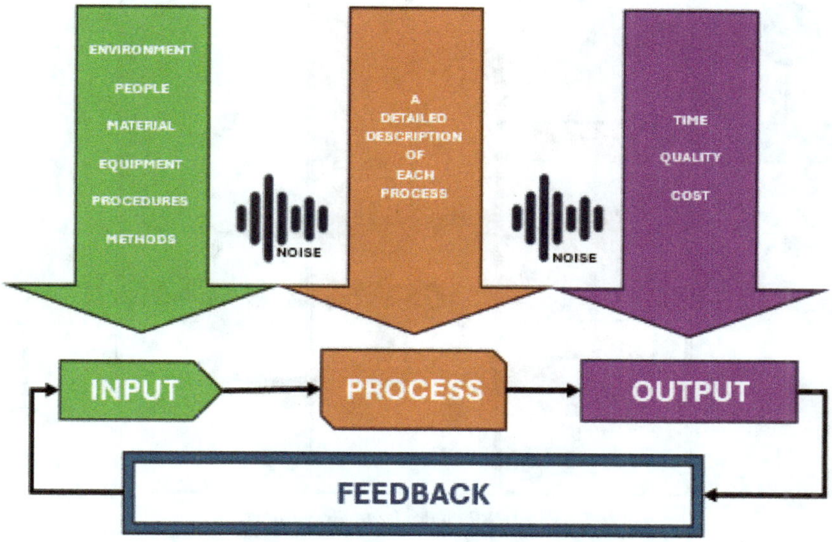

Figure 88. Input-Output (IPO) Analysis Technique

Wassily Leontief developed the input-output analysis and became a pivotal principle in economics.

This tool is used to visualize and analyze processes (from the SIPOC) by breaking them down into their key components. This works by illustrating the inputs to the process, the process itself, and the resulting outputs, which provide feedback on the variable that needs to change to improve the process in the next iteration.

It also allows for pinpointing the noise in the process that causes issues that show up as variation in a process.

Swim Lane Flow Chart

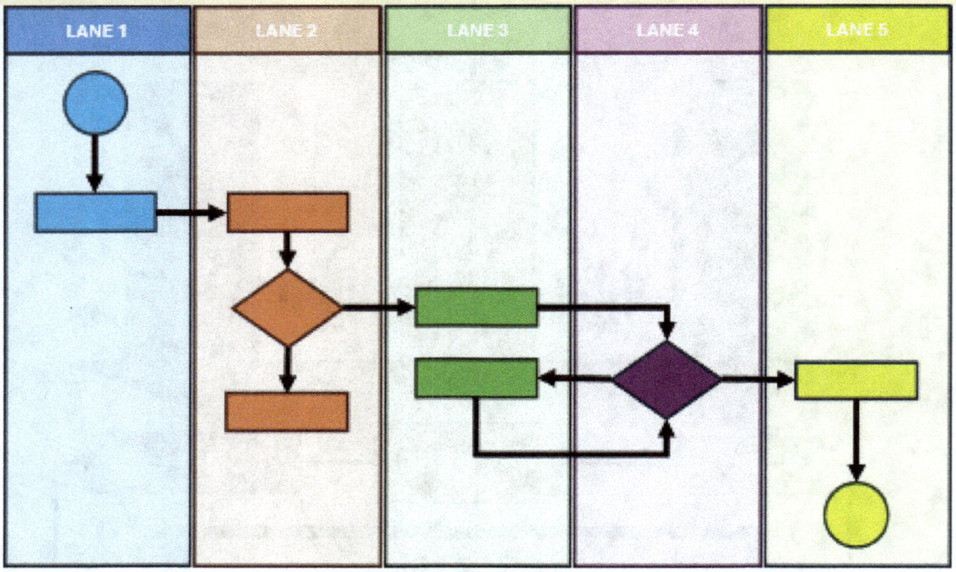

Figure 89. Swim Lane Flow Chart

A **Swim Lane Map** (also known as a **Swim Lane Diagram** or **Cross-Functional Flowchart**) is similar to a flowchart in that it visually maps out a process, its decisions, and its loops.

A swimlane map places events and actions in "lanes," usually by the person or department responsible for the work. The swim lanes distinguish how workers, teams, or departments within an organization carry out a specific task by placing activities, steps, interactions, and handoffs in the lane corresponding to the person taking the action.

The flow should always move down or to the right, with few loops. This type of chart is also helpful because you can add annotations and additional information right next to the flow or action itself.

Pareto Charts

Figure 90. Pareto Chart

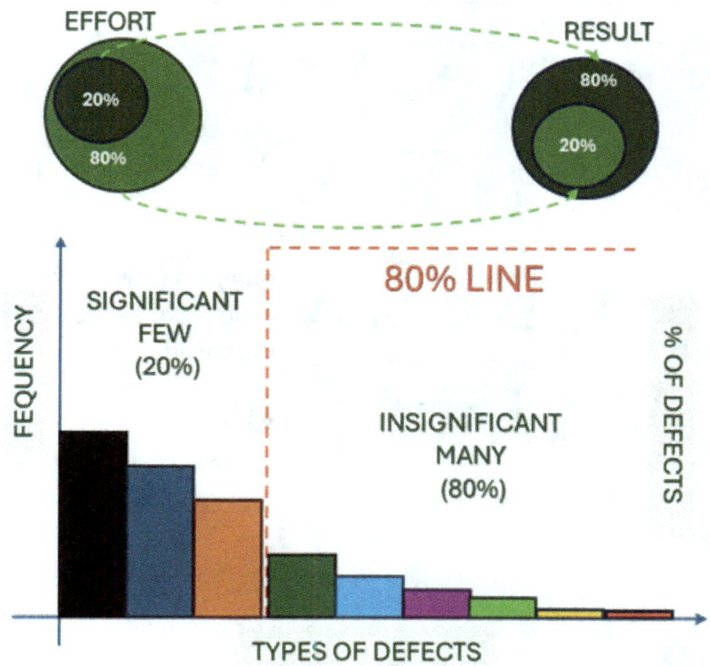

Pareto Analysis is typically used to prioritize issues, defects, or any elements that need attention. By focusing on the most critical causes, project managers can make efficient use of their resources to improve project performance.

Identify Problems or Causes: List all the problems or causes that need to be analyzed.

Measure Frequency or Impact: Quantify the frequency or impact of each problem.

Rank Problems: Rank the problems from most to least significant based on their frequency or impact.

Calculate Cumulative Impact: Identify which problems contribute most to the overall issue by calculating their cumulative impact.

Create a Pareto Chart: Plot a bar graph showing the problems in descending order of significance, along with a line graph showing the cumulative impact.

Critical to Quality Tree (CTQ Tree)

Figure 91. Critical to Quality Tree (CTQ Tree)

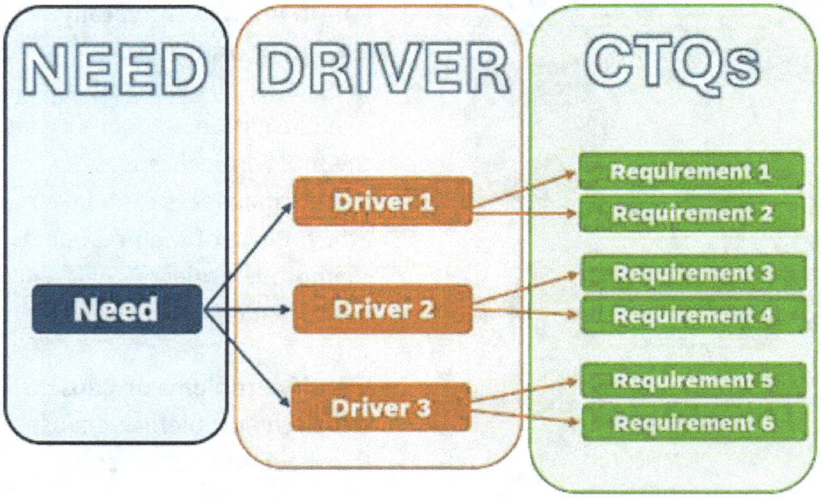

Need: The product or service that will be delivered in the project.

Drivers: Identify the qualities (drivers) for the product or service being delivered.

Requirements: What will be designed, developed, and delivered.

Step 1: Identify the customers.

Step 2: Solicit the **Voice of the Customer**.

Step 3: Understand customer needs.

Step 4: Translate that data into **Critical-to-Client** measures.

Step 5: Identify the **Quality Drivers**.

Step 6: Set parameters for your internal processes.

Step 7: Finally, validate the requirements.

Quality Function Deployment (QFD) - House of Quality (HOQ)

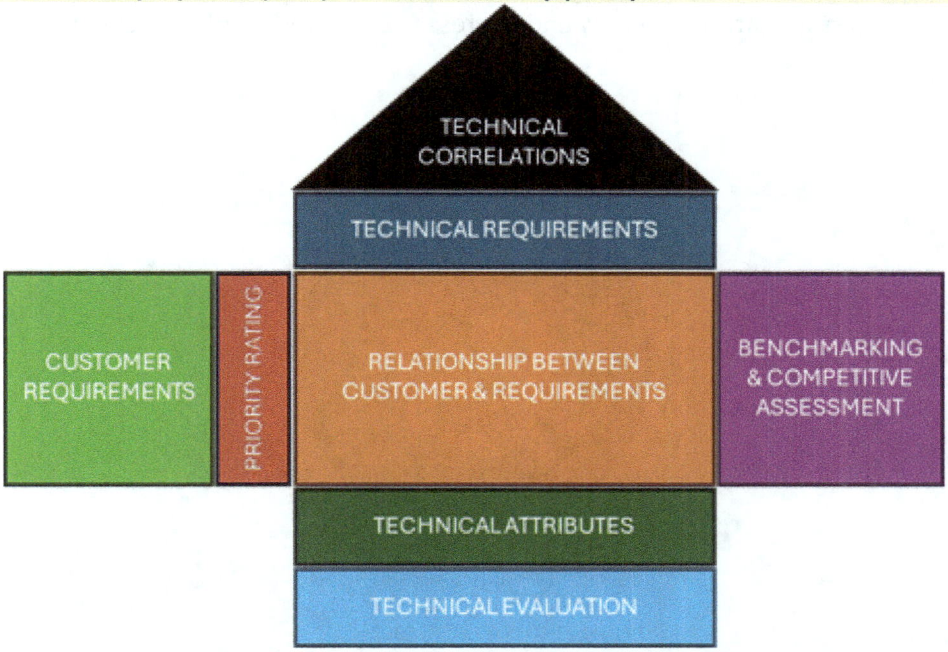

Figure 92. Quality Function Deployment (QFD) - House of Quality (HOQ)

The Quality Function Deployment, a structured approach for defining and translating customer requirements in the early stages of design, was developed in Japan in 1966 by Yoji Akao. QFD helps organize all customer needs and their design relationships into a matrix to understand better how they will be incorporated into the final product.

Step 1: Customer Requirements – "Voice of the Customer
Step 2: Technical measures
Step 3: Roof / Correlation Matrix
Step 4: Relationship Matrix
Step 5: Priority Rating
Step 6: Competitive Evaluation

Root Cause Analysis: Techniques such as the 5 Whys, fishbone diagrams, and fault tree analysis enable teams to systematically identify and address the root causes of project issues or defects.

5 Whys

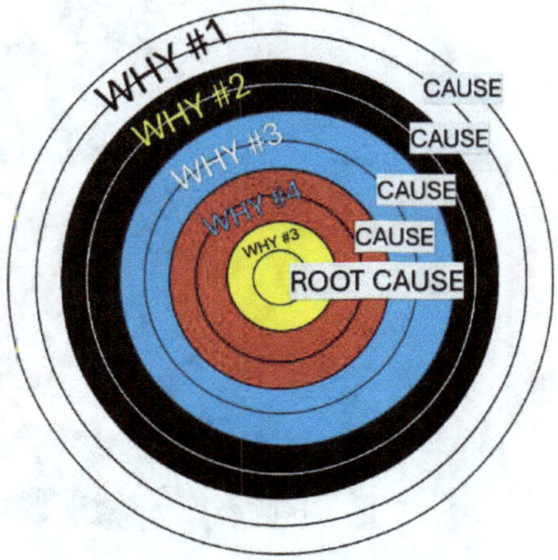

Figure 93. 5 Whys

In 1988, while at Toyota, Taiichi Ohno first used the 5 Whys to determine why a machine had stopped working and to solve project problems using a cause-and-effect approach, asking 'why' 5 times.

In most cases, you will get to the root of the problem before you ask the fifth why. Make sure you ask it as many times as needed to get to the root of the problem. One shortcoming of this method is failing to follow the process to reach the true root of the problem.

Fishbone Diagram

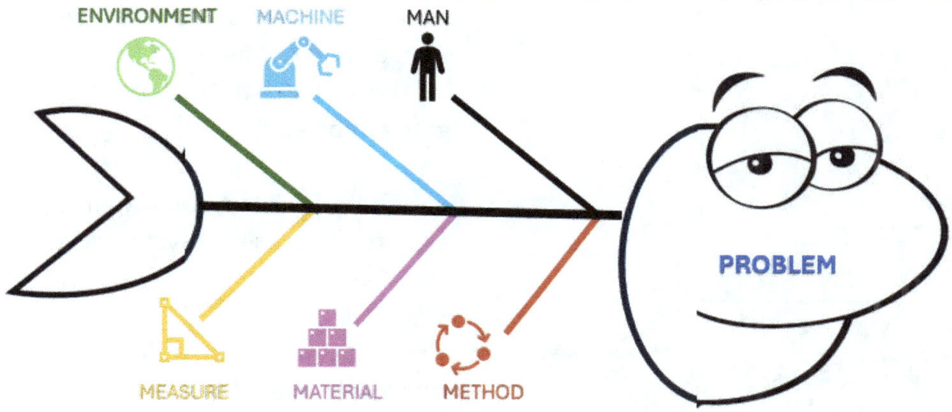

Figure 94. Fishbone Diagram

The goal is to find effective solutions to problems. A way to figure out what the actual causes of the problems you face are. Using this tool allows for early detection and stops the problem from recurring. The fishbone and other root cause analyses enable the problem to be pulled from the root rather than focusing only on the symptoms.

The problem is in the fish's head. The problem is what has gone wrong and/or continues to go wrong. The obvious or defined factors are on the main bones of the fish (environmental, machine, an, measure, material, and method). The 'why this happens' is in the smaller bones of the fish. These are the factors and subfactors. The next step is to figure out whether the 'whys' are:

> Casual: Output is dependent on present and past inputs, but not on future inputs.
> Non-casual: Output is dependent on present and past inputs as well as future inputs.

The potential impacts are also noted in the diagram.

Fault Tree Analysis

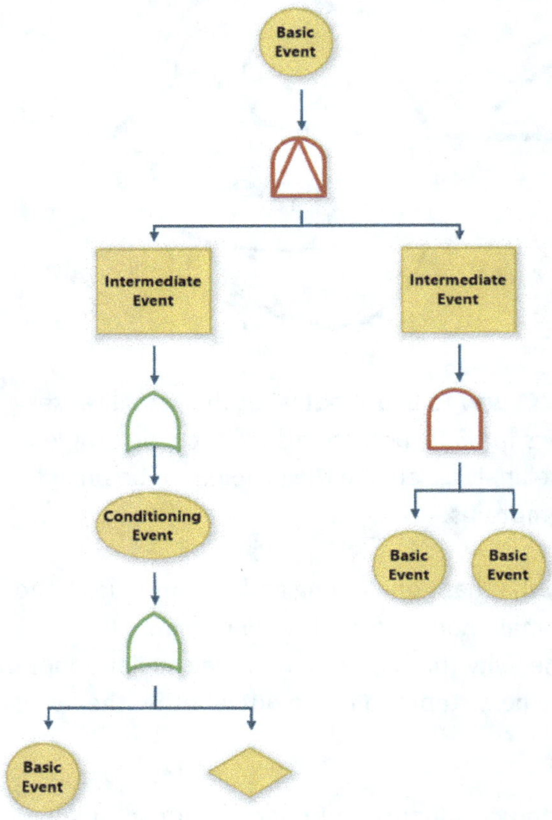

Figure 95. Fault Tree Analysis

Fault Tree Analysis was developed by H. Watson and A. Mearns in Bell Laboratories for the Air Force in 1962, using event and gate symbols.

This tool uses a top-down approach to explore the causes of system-level failures (The Basic Event).

The next step is to identify the causes of first-level system-level failures (Intermediate Events).

The logic gates (AND, OR gates), which connect the intermediate and basic events to identify the cause of the top undesired (basic) event.

Finally:

Calculate the probability of the lowest-level element occurrence

and

Measure the probabilities from the bottom up.

Data Analysis: Statistical tools such as histograms, Pareto charts, scatter plots, and control charts provide quantitative methods for analyzing project data, monitoring performance, and identifying areas for optimization. Used in Gap Analysis.

Histogram

PROJECTS ON TIME - SCHEDULE BY TYPE	
Project Type	**Number of Projects on Time**
Technology Projects	3
Business Projects	6
Internal Initiatives	1
Partnership Projects	8
Process Improvement Initiatives	6

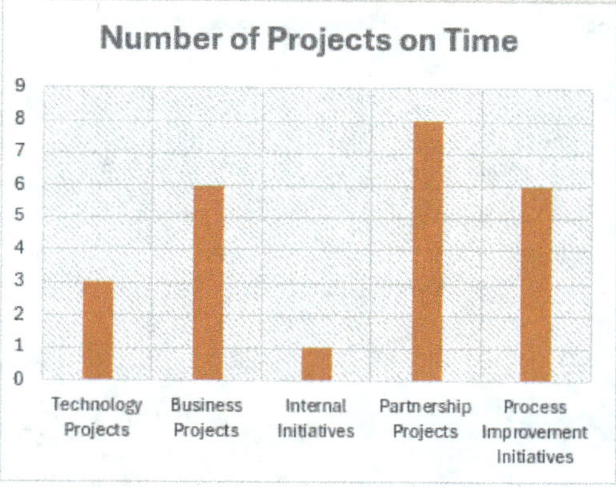

Figure 96. Histogram

This histogram is specifically a bar chart used for distributions of data (displaying the specific number) of projects that came in on time.

Karl Pearson, a Statistician, first coined the term histogram in 1892 in his lectures at the "Philosophical Transactions of the Royal Society of London". He defined the histograms "as a term for a common form of graphical representation, i.e., by columns marking as areas the frequency corresponding to the range of their base."

The bars of a histogram represent continuous data for a specific range, measured in terms of frequencies and intervals; thus, the bars are connected.

Scatter Plot Diagram

Project Type	Number of Projects Behind Schedule	Number of Projects on
Technology Projects	2	3
Business Projects	3	6
Internal Initiatives	8	1
Partnership Projects	6	8
Process Improvement Initiatives	2	6

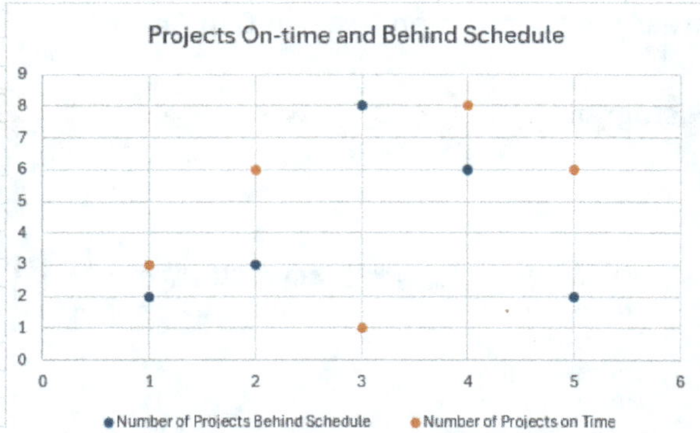

Figure 101. Scatter Plot Diagram

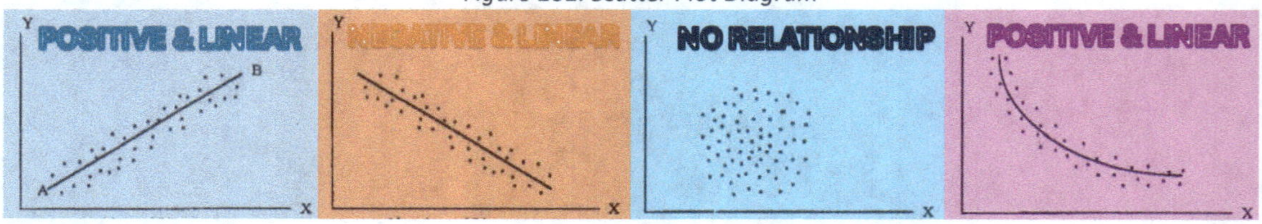

Each dot on the horizontal and vertical axes represents the values for an individual data point. The dots represent two different variables and are usually colored differently.

Shows the relationships between two numeric variables. Relationships between variables can be described in many ways: positive or negative, strong or weak, linear or nonlinear. It is common to add a trend line to the plot that shows the best-fitting mathematical model to the data.

We can also observe outlier points, which lie outside the cluster and require further investigation.

Control Chart

DATE	MEASUREMENT	MEAN	UCL (3σ)	LCL (3σ)
2/1/2024	17	15.52	25.3246227	5.70986002
2/2/2024	12	15.52	25.3246227	5.70986002
2/3/2024	20	15.52	25.3246227	5.70986002
2/4/2024	13	15.52	25.3246227	5.70986002
2/5/2024	13	15.52	25.3246227	5.70986002
2/6/2024	18	15.52	25.3246227	5.70986002
2/7/2024	16	15.52	25.3246227	5.70986002
2/8/2024	17	15.52	25.3246227	5.70986002
2/9/2024	17	15.52	25.3246227	5.70986002
2/10/2024	12	15.52	25.3246227	5.70986002
2/11/2024	11	15.52	25.3246227	5.70986002
2/12/2024	20	15.52	25.3246227	5.70986002
2/13/2024	12	15.52	25.3246227	5.70986002
2/14/2024	17	15.52	25.3246227	5.70986002
2/15/2024	19	15.52	25.3246227	5.70986002
2/16/2024	20	15.52	25.3246227	5.70986002
2/17/2024	13	15.52	25.3246227	5.70986002
2/18/2024	13	15.52	25.3246227	5.70986002
2/19/2024	18	15.52	25.3246227	5.70986002
2/20/2024	16	15.52	25.3246227	5.70986002
2/21/2024	17	15.52	25.3246227	5.70986002
2/22/2024	17	15.52	25.3246227	5.70986002
2/23/2024	12	15.52	25.3246227	5.70986002
2/24/2024	20	15.52	25.3246227	5.70986002
2/25/2024	11	15.52	25.3246227	5.70986002
2/26/2024	20	15.52	25.3246227	5.70986002
2/27/2024	12	15.52	25.3246227	5.70986002

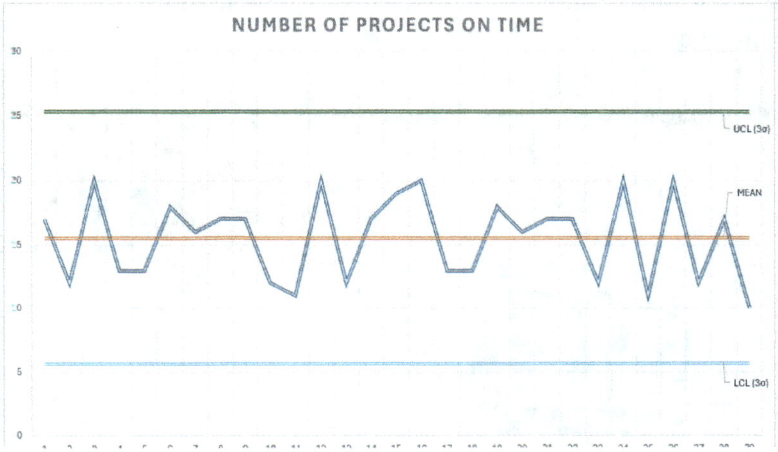

Figure 97. Control Chart

The purpose of a control chart is to monitor process results over time.

There is an optimal space for a process – meaning the process is operating as designed. There are times when a process overperforms and times when it encounters problems, leading to suboptimal effectiveness. The results of the process are charted, and the variation out of the normal range in the process is divided into two types: **Common cause of variation** is the "natural" variation in the process. It is the natural variation in the process. It is consistent and predictable. **Special cause of variation** is not supposed to be there. You want to identify the reasons for special causes of variation and prevent them from recurring.

The first results provide the estimated mean and standard deviation. The X control chart, shown in the tables and chart, includes:

UCL (Upper Control Limit): The green line
Center Line (Goal): the red line
LCL (Lower Control Limit): The blue line

Lean Tools: Methods such as 5S (Sort, Straighten, Shine, Standardize, Sustain), Kanban boards, and Kaizen events promote continuous improvement and streamline project workflows by eliminating waste and non-value-added activities.

5S (Sort, Straighten, Shine, Standardize, Sustain)

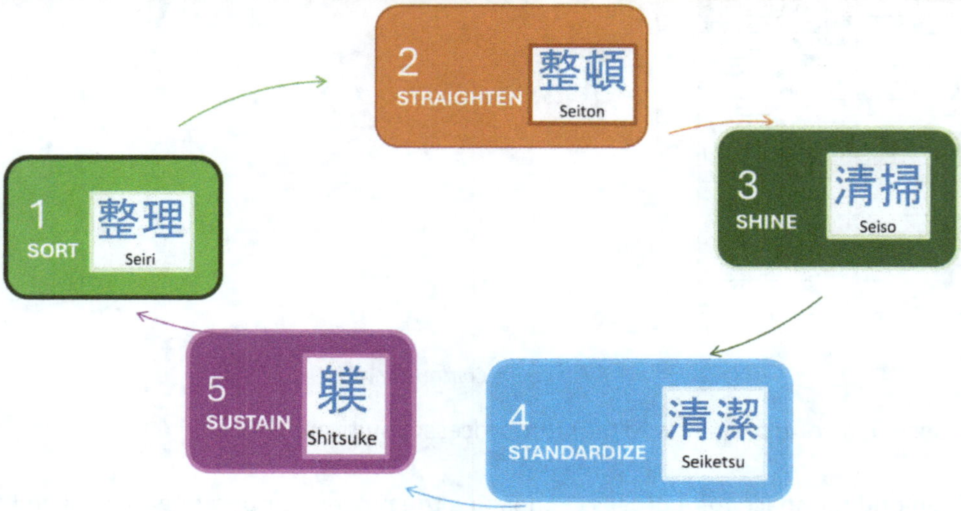

Figure 98. 5S (Sort, Straighten, Shine, Standardize, Sustain)

The steps in organizing and maintaining a clean, efficient, and safe workspace. The goal of this lean method is to ensure that the workspace is clean, uncluttered, and does not waste time or cause injury—lean is based on the original Japanese: seiri, seiton, seiso, seiketsu, and shitsuke.

Sort (seiri): Workers *sort* everything in a workspace into what is and what is not needed, using "red tagging".
Straighten (Seiton): Workers position items based on frequency of use.
Shine (Seiso): Workers clean their stations every day and throughout the day
Standardize (Seiketsu): How to sustain the work of the first three steps.
Sustain (Shitsuke): Developing new standards and building standard operating procedures for upkeep.

Kanban Board

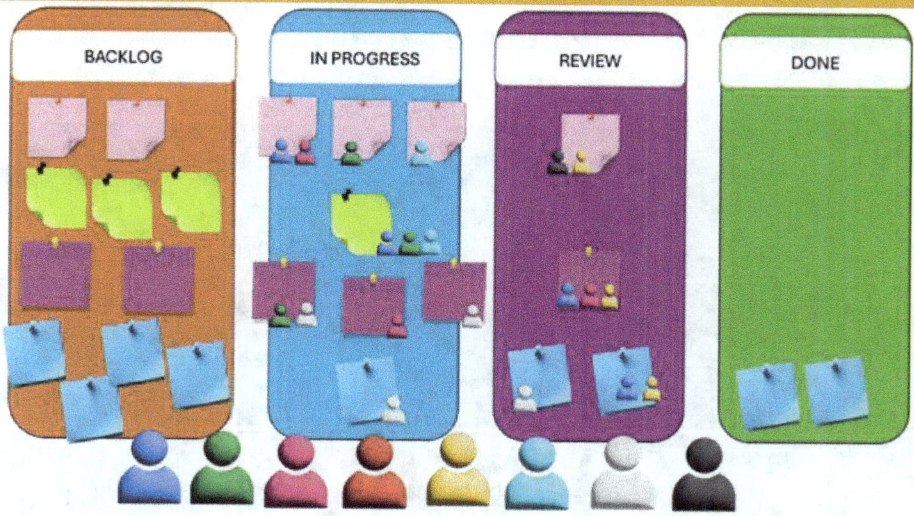

Figure 99. Kanban Board

Project teams find that visualizing how their workflows provide organization, context, and transparency. Kanban was initially created in the 1940s by Taiichi Ohno as a part of lean manufacturing. Lean and other Six Sigma concepts will be discussed in detail later in the book.

An Agile board can range from a low-tech whiteboard with sticky notes to a high-tech project management application that shows the current sprint's user stories and progress.

It comprises columns representing the stages of work, and sticky notes, cards, etc., represent the work as it moves through the project management process. Each card represents a task from the backlog assigned to a person or group. Many management methods flow from manufacturing, and Kanban did too.

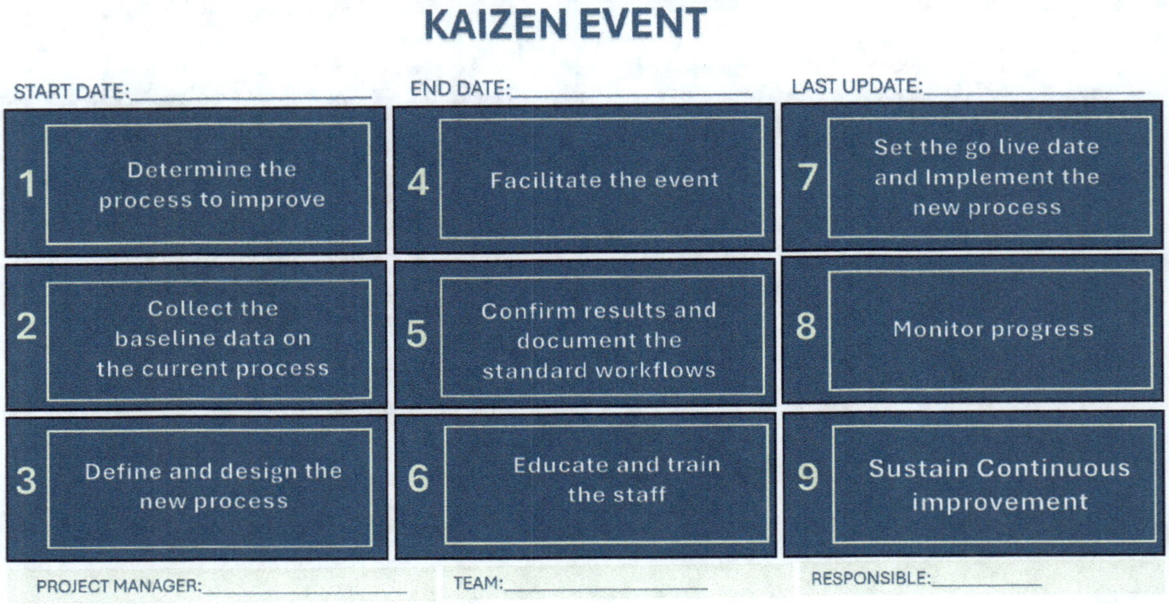

Figure 100. Kaizen Event

What is it?

Focuses on eliminating the eight wastes in a process.

Who Participates?

Anyone with knowledge and a stake in the process under discussion should be sure to be drawn in at all levels of the organization.

When should they happen?

Whenever waste needs to be removed from a process or operation, or when the process is not working as planned, it is necessary to get to the root of the problem.

Project Risk Analysis and Management: Proactively identifying and responding to risks that could affect the outcomes of a project.

FMEA – Failure Mode and Effects Analysis

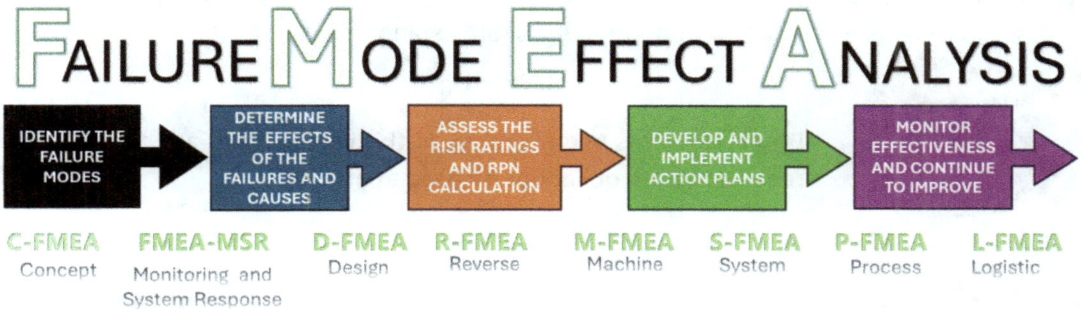

Figure 101. FMEA – Failure Mode and Effects Analysis

In the 1940s, the military developed the failure mode and effects analysis (FMEA) to identify, prioritize, and resolve failures.

Failure Mode: the way or mode in which a process might fail.
Effects Analysis: the consequences of failures.

Failures are prioritized by their risk priority number (RPN):

RPN = S x O x D - The Scales are from one to 10

- **Severity (S)**: The seriousness of their consequences - 1 is insignificant and 10 is catastrophic.
- **Occurrence (O):** The likelihood of a specific failure mode happening - 1 is highly unlikely and 10 is almost inevitable.
- **Detection (D):** How easily a failure can be detected before it becomes a problem. The higher the score, the more difficult it is to detect.

Waste Elimination: Taiichi Ohno, in the Toyota Production System, defined three areas of waste: non-value-adding activities (mura), overburden (muri), and waste (muda).

8 Wastes *Table 12. 8 Wastes*

Defects, Overproduction, waiting, non-utilized talent, transportation, inventory, motion, and extra processing. Defects – Products that don't meet quality standards.

Defects – Errors and Mistakes. In this waste, items are created that either require rework or cannot be used at all.

Overproduction – Exceeding demand or producing more than was ordered. In this waste, doing work or creating items before they are needed or requested.

Waiting – the lag time between steps in production. In this situation, employees are left waiting for what they need to do their work. At this time, no value is being added.

Non-Utilized Talent – Ineffectively using or miscalculating human resources. In this waste, employees are not used to the fullest extent of their abilities.

Transportation – Inefficient shipping methods. In this waste, items are moved more than necessary, whether in the building or on the road.

Inventory – Holding on to a surplus of product or raw material, resulting in waste, not following the rules of Just In Time (JIT), and having items on the shelf that a customer has not requested.

Motion – Unnecessary moving of product, material, or people. In this waste, any movement that does not directly contribute to the work at hand is considered.

Overprocessing – Doing more work than is needed in a very inefficient manner. In this waste, processing that does not add value to the item as originally designed.

The Three M's—MUDA, MURA, MURI — are terms often used together in the Toyota Production System.

Table 15. MUDA, MURA, MURI

MUDA - OVERBURDENED

MURA - INCONSISTENCY

MURI - WASTEFULNESS

SIX SIGMA AND THE ORGANIZATION

Lean Six Sigma in project management focuses on continuous refinement, client-centricity, and statistics-backed decisions. Project administrators thereby enhance planning, execution, oversight, and results by using data-backed information in their decision-making.

Adaptable techniques underpin continuous advantage by optimizing information processing, participants' acumen, and receptiveness to constant alignment. Quality in project management remains an ever-evolving journey.

While project management and Lean Six Sigma are technically distinct methodologies, they can also work hand in hand to improve an organization's success. And even more, by incorporating additional methods such as Agile and Scrum for further improvement.

Culture

A major consideration is the collocated team. Many project teams are made up of team members from different time zones and cultures. Organizations have deployed tools that allow for projects to be managed virtually. Many of the tools support virtual calls and meetings, document sharing, and AI transcription and summarization. Being agile not only with the work of the project, but also in how we work. Using a one-size-fits-all approach is an absolute recipe for disaster in the fast-moving projects that require it.

Roles and Responsibilities

Table 13. Six Sigma Roles and Responsibilities

Champion	An executive who sponsors the project and owns the vision, direction, and business results. They are responsible for leading change and own the value streams.
Project Sponsor	Owns the improvement plan, financial results, and removes barriers.
Process Owners	Maybe Process Owners. Captures the metrics, owns the communication and deployment plans.
Team Member	They are usually part-time participants on projects from teams specific to the work being performed. The Subject Matter Experts (SMEs) and Stakeholders
Facilitator	A Green or Black Belt who leads the work of the project, similar to a project manager in traditional projects or a scrum master in Agile.

Team Types

Ad Hoc Teams are assembled to complete one short-term project. The Team's skills are specific to the project.

Cellular Teams are decentralized, composed of a permanent core of team members and people from different business units, with a set of skills spanning multiple domains.

Cross-functional Teams are made up of workers from different departments. Usually, the skills and knowledge sets are specialized for the specific project.

Parallel Teams are two teams working on the same project, often supporting each other.

Self-directed Teams operate with minimal management oversight and direction. They determine all aspects of project objectives and work.

Team Dynamics and Performance

An important part of a successful Six Sigma project is a team that works well together to complete the work efficiently and effectively. In 1965, Bruce Tuckman introduced the five stages of team development. It is imperative for the project's health that the team reach the performing stage in good order; otherwise, the project is likely doomed.

Table 14. The 5 Stages of Team Development

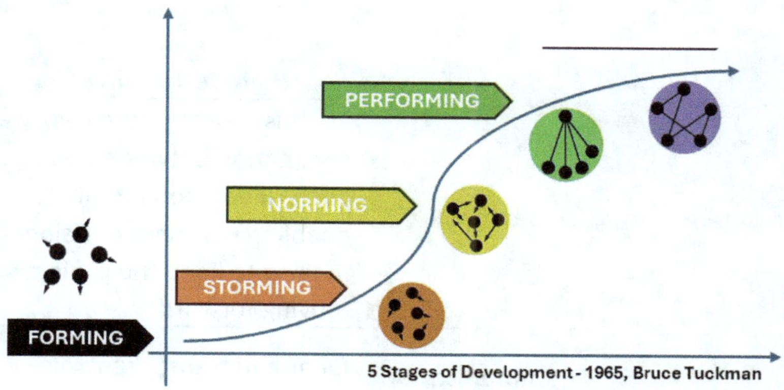

- **Forming** - team development kicks off with the Forming stage, where everyone figures out their roles and how the group's going to work together;
- **Storming** - some conflict and competition as everyone's roles and the team's rhythm start to take shape;
- **Norming** -brings about consolidation as participants begin to resolve their differences, appreciate colleagues' strengths, and respect the team roles;
- **Performing** - high levels of cooperation, coordination, and productivity; and
- **Adjourning** - tie up loose ends, reflect on the journey, and give a big shout-out to everyone for their hard work.

High and Low Performing Six Sigma Teams

Table 15. High and Low Performing Six Sigma Teams

	High-Performing Teams	Low-Performing Teams
Dependence	Trust is rooted in the clarity and connection between managers and skilled team members, enabling real-time decision-making to keep the project moving forward.	Highly dependent on top-down management. The team does not have the freedom to make decisions in real time to keep the project on track without intervention.
Communication	Clear and transparent communication channels.	Intermittent or absent communication channels.
Conflict	Have incorporated and follow the procedures to solve conflicts that arise during the life of the project. Often, there is a strong project manager who does not let conflict escalate.	Possibly stuck in the storming stage, or cannot solve the issues that arise, so they don't negatively affect the progress of the project. Often absent is a Project Manager who de-escalates conflict.
Support	They are fully supported by Management, culturally, with the resources and money needed to be successful.	Have insufficient backing or support from management to be successful.

Business Results for Projects

Projects are the vehicles for improvements within the organization. Projects are initiated because the organization wants to enhance or improve its internal capabilities. This may be through improving or replacing the current system, or by bringing in a new system to fill a gap. In the business case and feasibility studies, pertinent questions are asked and investigated. The goal is to ensure that organizational processes perform well and can meet the elicited requirements. The goal of requirements is to improve efficiency, effectiveness, and quality of the processes, systems, or applications under scrutiny.

In traditional project management, the initiation phase starts the project management lifecycle. With Six Sigma, it is the Define Phase. Much of the same work is conducted, including understanding the project's purpose and scope, customer expectations, timelines, and costs. Where six sigma becomes a powerful project management tool is that it also examines the process, or the lack of one. During the Define phase, the project manager will ensure that current processes are mapped to establish the project and fulfill its true purpose.

During this time, the Sponsor's goal is to achieve the desired results while minimizing variation, and must have a plan to address outputs that exceed the organization's appetite for variation. To move to data-supported information, the following path is suggested:

Goals and Objectives: Define the objectives from the outset by establishing clear, measurable goals aligned with the organizational strategies that underpin the initiative or project.

Key Processes: Identify and examine the processes that influence achieving the defined project objectives.

Measures and Metrics: Identify the metrics that specifically gauge the product's performance under development.

Data: Choose data measures that improve problem-solving and benchmarking, and that assist in achieving excellence. Investigate and report how the data for the identified measures will be collected, ensuring the data is accurate and timely.

Resources: Understanding the resources, both human and otherwise, that can be dedicated to the endeavor underway.

Schedule: How long will it realistically take to complete the project? It is important to create realistic timelines that account for the amount of work already on the human resources department's plate needed to complete the project.

Benchmarking: Comparing a company's performance with industry best practices or competitors to identify areas for improvement.

Data and Key Performance Indicators

Collecting Data Collection: Where does the data reside to get the answers that will be needed for the project? Who will supply the data to the project? How often will it be delivered? Having the outline of the data collection process is an essential part of project planning.

Key Performance Indicators (KPIs): There is variation in every process. Not all variation is negative, and not all of it should be tracked. Track and encourage progress on the organization's critical goals. Every project should, at a minimum, track delays, defects, dissatisfaction, and dollars.

Process Performance

Process performance refers to how well a process is currently operating, measured by speed, efficiency, and quality metrics. PpK is the Process Performance Index that measures how much a process varies and how consistently it meets the requirements for the project or initiative. This statistic can be used throughout the project lifecycle to ensure that the new or improved system is indeed making the improvements the organization desires. The measures of major importance in measuring process performance that should be constantly under examination are:

Table 16. Process Performance

Efficiency	How well time, money, and materials are utilized in a process. The goal is to maximize the output while minimizing waste.
Effectiveness	The ability of a process to achieve its intended purpose. Being effective means delivering outcomes consistent with the defined objectives.
Quality	The standard of the outputs produced by a process is meeting or exceeding customer expectations, while adhering to requirements and ensuring the results are free from defects.
Error Rate	The frequency at which errors occur in the application. A good vs. acceptable error rate will vary depending on the application, use case, and your users' expectations.
Cycle Time	The total time from start to finish of a process. A shorter cycle time reflects a well-optimized process.
Throughput	The rate at which a process produces output within a specific time.
Yield	The percentage of defect-free output compared to the total number of units processed. This is the number of correct outputs divided by the total number of outputs; a higher yield indicates a more successful process.
Customer Satisfaction	Assessing Customer satisfaction via feedback on the process outcomes they experience.

How Lean Six Sigma Enhances Project Workflows

Lean Six Sigma project management helps project teams identify bottlenecks and eliminate activities that don't add value to project outcomes by:

Ordinary project wastes include delays between project phases, creating deliverables before they're needed, and rework due to quality issues that could have been prevented. Value stream mapping visualizes project workflows to identify inefficiencies and bottlenecks. Kanban boards set work-in-progress limits to prevent overloading team members, while poka-yoke techniques mistake-proof project processes.

Control charts graph process performance over time, with upper and lower control limits that indicate when processes are operating normally or experiencing unusual variation. These visual tools help project managers spot problems before they impact deliverables.

Basic statistical concepts include the mean (average performance), the standard deviation (how much the data spreads from the average), and process capability (how well a process meets specifications). Understanding these measurements helps teams maintain consistent project quality.

Process mapping creates visual documentation of project workflows, making it easier to spot inefficiencies and improvement opportunities. These maps show how workflows flow from one stage to the next and where delays typically occur.

Make Six Sigma part of regular project routines by integrating quality checkpoints into existing project phases. Consistently measuring quality should become a habit rather than a separate activity that adds extra work to team schedules. Build quality gates into project workflows that require teams to meet specific criteria before moving to the next phase. This prevents defects from accumulating and reduces the need for extensive rework later in the project lifecycle.

These actionable Six Sigma techniques can be implemented immediately to solve real project management challenges and improve outcomes.

Challenges and Success Factors

Implementing Lean Six Sigma in project management is not without its challenges. One major hurdle is gaining buy-in and support from leadership and team members. Lean Six Sigma requires a cultural shift and commitment to continuous improvement, which can be challenging to instill across an organization. Proper training is crucial to ensure everyone understands the principles, tools, and techniques involved.

Another challenge lies in selecting the right projects and areas to apply Lean Six Sigma methodology. It works best for repeatable, process-driven projects rather than unique, creative initiatives. Identifying key processes ripe for optimization requires careful analysis. Inadequate process metrics and data can also hinder effective Lean Six Sigma deployment.

Despite the challenges, many organizations have realized immense success by combining Lean Six Sigma with project management. Critical success factors include:

Top-Down Leadership Support: Visible endorsement and participation from executive leadership provide legitimacy and resources.

Proper Training: Investing in comprehensive Six Sigma belts training and certifications equips teams with the skills to succeed.

Data-Driven Decision Making: Lean Six Sigma's reliance on data ensures fact-based process improvements rather than operating based on assumptions.

Continuous Improvement Mindset: Embracing the philosophy of constantly identifying and eliminating waste and defects drives long-term optimization.

Project Selection: Focusing Lean Six Sigma efforts on high-impact processes maximizes the return on investment.

Lean Six Sigma List of Terms

Sometimes you just need a good list.

Table 17. Lean Six Sigma List of Terms

A	B	C
1. A3 2. Action Plan 3. Affinity Chart (Affinity Diagram) 4. Agile 5. Ally's Network Worksheet 6. Alternative Path 7. Alternative Hypothesis 8. Analyze Phase 9. Anderson-Darling Test for Normality 10. Andon 11. ANOVA 12. Approvals 13. Assumption Busting 14. Attribute Data (Discrete Data) 15. Autonomation (Jidoka) 16. Average (Mean)	17. Balanced Scorecard 18. Bartlett's Test 19. Baseline Measures 20. Batching 21. Best Practice Sharing (Yokoten) 22. Black Belt 23. Black Belt Project Storyboard 24. Black Belt Tollgate Checklist 25. Bottleneck 26. Box Plot (Box and Whisker Plot) 27. Brainstorming 28. Business Case	29. C Chart 30. Catchball 31. Cause and Effect Diagram 32. Central Tendency 33. Champion (Sponsor) 34. Changeover Reduction 35. Changeover Time 36. Check Sheet 37. Chi-Square Test 38. Coaching Kata (Coaching Practice) 39. Coaching Questions 40. Cockpit Chart (Dashboard) 41. Common Cause Variation 42. Comparative Analysis 43. Contingent Actions 44. Continuous Data (Variable Data) 45. Continuous Improvement 46. Control Phase 47. Control Chart 48. Control Chart Decision Tree

C	D	E
49. Control Plan 50. Correlation Coefficient (Pearson Correlation) 51. Cost/Benefit Analysis 52. Cost of Poor Quality (COPQ) 53. Countermeasure 54. Critic's Club Worksheet 55. Critical-to-Quality 56. Crosby's 14 Steps to Quality Improvement 57. Cross-Training 58. Cross-Functional Flowchart (Deployment or Swimlane Map) 59. Customer 60. Customer Focus 61. Customer Journey Mapping 62. Customer Requirements 63. Customer Value 64. Cycle Time	70. Dashboard (Cockpit Chart) 71. Data Analysis 72. Data Collection Plan 73. Decisions 74. Defect 75. Design Project 76. Discrete Data (Attribute Data) 77. Dispersion 78. DMAIC 79. DMADV 80. DOE – One Factor At A Time (OFAT) 81. DOE (Design of Experiments) 82. DOE – Full Factorial 83. DOE – Fractional Factorial 84. Documentation 85. Downstream 86. Defects per Million Opportunities (DPMO) 87. Defects per Opportunity (DPO) 88. Defect Opportunity 89. Defective 90. Define Phase 91. Demand Levelling 92. Deployment Map (Swimlane Map or Cross-Functional Chart)	93. Effectiveness 94. Efficiency 95. Efficiency & Effectiveness Matrix 96. Executive Summary 97. Extra-Processing 98. External Failure

F	G	H
99. Facilitator 100. Failure Modes & Effects Analysis (FMEA) 101. Fishbone Diagram (Cause & Effect Diagram) 102. Flow 103. Flow Chart (Process Map) 104. Focus Groups 105. The Four Absolutes of Quality 106. Force Field Analysis Future State Map	109. Gallery Walk 110. Gemba (Workplace) 111. Gemba Board (Process Walk Board) 112. Gemba Walk (Process Walk) 113. Gemba Walk Interview Sheet (Process Walk Interview Sheet) 114. Goal Statement Green Belt	115. Handoff 116. Heijunka (Production Leveling) 117. Help-Hinder 118. Hidden Plant 119. Histogram 120. Historical Parameters 121. Hoshin Kanri (Policy Deployment) 122. Huddle Meeting 123. Hypothesis Statement Hypothesis Test Decision Tree
I	**J**	**L**
124. I & MR Chart (X & MR or Chart) 125. Implementation Plan 126. Improve Phase 127. Impact/Effort Matrix 128. Improvement Kata (Toyota Kata, Improvement Practice) 129. Infrastructure Project 130. Input 131. Input Measures 132. Institutionalization 133. Inspections 134. Internal Failure 135. Inventory	136. Jidoka (Autonomation) 137. Juran's Trilogy 138. Just-In-Time (JIT) **K** 149. Kaizen Event 150. Kamishibai Boards (Leader Task Boards) 151. Kanban (Signboard) 152. Kanban Board 153. Kano Model	139. Lead Time 140. Leader Huddle Meetings 141. Leader Process Walks 142. Leader Standard Work (LSW) 143. Leader Task Boards (Kamishibai Boards) 144. Lean 145. Lean Culture 146. Lean Six Sigma 147. Levene's Test 148. Line Balancing Load Leveling (Heijunka)

M	N	O
154. Management By Fact	175. New Procedure Audit	181. Obstacle Parking Lot
155. Mann-Whitney Test	176. Non-Utilized Talent	182. One Proportion Test
156. Master Black Belt	177. Non-Value-Adding Activities	183. One-Sample Sign Test
157. Matching X & Y Measures	178. Normality Test (Anderson-Darling Test for Normality)	184. One-Sample T-Test
158. Mean (Average)	179. nP Chart	185. One-Way ANOVA
159. Measure Phase	180. Null Hypothesis	186. Operational Definition
160. Measurement Selection Matrix		187. Opportunity
161. Measurement Systems Analysis (MSA, Gage R&R)		188. Output
162. Median		189. Output Measures
163. Meeting & Project Roles		190. Overall Equipment Effectiveness (OEE)
164. Mistake Proofing (Poka-yoke)		191. Overproduction
165. Mode		
166. Moment of Truth		
167. Monitoring & Response Plan		
168. Mood's Median Test		
169. Motion		
170. MSA – Continuous Data (Gage R&R – Continuous)		
171. MSA – Discrete Data (Gage R&R – Discrete)		
172. Muda (Waste)		
173. Multi-Voting		
174. Multiple Regression Test		

P	P	P
193. P Chart 194. P-Value 195. Parallel Processing 196. Pareto Chart 197. Pareto Principle 198. PDCA/PDSA 199. Percent Complete & Accurate 200. Perfection 201. Pilot 202. Plus/Delta 203. PMO (Project Management Office) 204. Poka-yoke (Mistake Proofing) 205. Policy Deployment (Hoshin Kanri) 206. Pose & Answer 207. Preliminary Plan 208. Preventive Action 209. Problem Statement 210. Process 211. Process Analysis 212. Process Capability 192.	213. Process Capability for Continuous Data (Process Capability Indicators) 214. Process Improvement 215. Process Improvement Project 216. Process Management 217. Process Map (Flow Chart) 218. Process Measures 219. Process Owner 220. Process Partners 221. Process Performance Boards 222. Process Redesign 223. Process Redesign & Reengineering 224. Process Sigma 225. Process Sponsor 226. Process Time 193.	227. Process Voices 228. Process Walk (Gemba Walk) 229. Process Walk Board (Gemba Board) 230. Process Walk Interview Sheet (Gemba Walk Interview Sheet) 231. Production Leveling (Heijunka) 232. Project Charter 233. Project Closure 234. Project Management Office (PMO) 235. Project Scope 236. Project Selection 237. Project Selection Guide 238. Project Y 239. Proportion Defective 240. Pull
Q	**R**	**R**
241. Quality 242. Quartile 243. Quick Win	244. RACI 245. Range 246. Rapid Improvement Event (Kaizen) 247. Red Tag 248. Redundancy 249. Regression Test 250. Repeatability 251. Reproducibility	252. Rework Loop 253. Risk Management 254. Rolled Throughput Yield (YRT) 255. Root Cause Analysis 256. Root Cause Hypothesis 257. R&R 258. Run Chart (Time Series Plot)

S	S	S
258. Sampling 259. Sampling Bias 260. Sampling Calculations 261. Scatter Plot 262. Scientific Method 263. Scope (Project Scope) 264. Scrum 265. Scrum Team 266. Seiketsu (Standardize) 267. Seiri (Sort) 268. Seiso (Shine) 269. Seiton (Set in Order) 270. Set in Order (Seiton) 271. Setup Reduction 272. Seven Basic Quality Tools 273.	274. Shadow Board 275. Shine (Seiso) 276. Shitsuke (Sustain) 277. Single-Piece-Flow 278. SIPOC 279. Six Sigma 280. SMED (Single Minute Exchange of Die) 281. Solution Parking Lot 282. Solution Selection Matrix 283. Sort (Seiri) 284. Spaghetti Map 285. Special Cause Variation 286. Statistical Process Control (SPC) 287. Stakeholder 288. Stakeholder Analysis 289. Standard Deviation 290. Standard Work	291. Standard Operating Procedure (SOP) 292. Standardize (Seiketsu) 293. Stop-Start-Continue 294. Storyboard 295. Stratification 296. Subject Matter Expert 297. Supermarket 298. Supplier 299. Survey 300. Sustain (Shitsuke) 301. Swimlane Map (Deployment Map or Cross-Functional Chart)
T	**T**	**T**
302. Taguchi Loss Function 303. Taguchi Methods 304. Takt Time 305. Target 306. Task Board 307. Team Alignment Diagnostic 308. Test for Two Variances(F-Test) 309. Theory of Constraints (aka TOC) 310. Threats & Opportunities Matrix 311. Time Analysis 312.	313. Time Series Plot (Run Chart) 314. To-Be Maps 315. TOC (Theory of Constraints) 316. Total Quality Control (TQC) 317. Total Quality Management (TQM) 318. Toyota Production System (TPS) 319. Toyota's 8 Steps for Practical Problem Solving 320. TPS (Toyota Production System)	321. TQM (Total Quality Management) 322. Transportation (Touches) 323. Tree Diagram 324. True North 325. TQC (Total Quality Control) 326. Two Proportions Test 327. Two Sample T-Test

U	V	W
328. U Chart 329. Upstream	330. Value-Added Flow Analysis 331. Value Adding Activities 332. Value Analysis 333. Value Enabling Activities 334. Value Stream Map 335. Variation 336. Visual Management 337. Visual Workplace 338. VOC Translation Matrix 339. Voice of the Customer (VOC)	340. Wait Time 341. Waiting 342. Waste Walk 343. Water Beetle (or Water Spider) 344. Weighted Criteria Matrix 345. White Belt 346. WIP(Work-In-Process) 347. Work Cell Design 348. Work-In-Process (WIP) 349. Workload Balancing
X	**Y**	**Z**
350. X-Bar & R Charts 351. X-Bar & S Charts	352. Y=f(x) 353. Yellow Belt 354. Yield 355. Yokoten (Best Practice Sharing)	356. Zero Defects 357. Zero Quality Control

CHAPTER FIVE: BRINGING THEM ALL TOGETHER

The Trifecta of managing today's complex projects includes: The Project Management Body of Knowledge, Agile Practices, and the Six Sigma Framework.

In this chapter, you will:

Review how the Project Management Body of Knowledge, Agile Practices, and the Six Sigma Framework work together to allow for a 360-degree management of projects.

You have learned the tools required to manage a project from initiation through closure. You now have the tools, techniques, and templates to hit the ground running as a new project manager or a refresher if you are seasoned in the field. The chapter on project management was very detailed, but you should be able to take what you need to be successful, given that all projects are unique.

Learning to be Agile and not just go through the motions of the steps to do Agile. Learning the Agile manifesto and the declaration of interdependence, and how that lines up with your projects, is a great place to start. But there is much more to do. The chapter on Agile introduced the most common flavors of Agile, along with lesser-known methodologies that will definitely help you structure your projects for success.

The way projects are managed now considers new ways of working and all of the tools we have around us. Project Managers have adopted hybrid agile project management approaches, tools, and techniques. Overlaying the DMAIC phases over the project management lifecycle is a game-changer. The Project Management Phase — monitoring and controlling — tells the project manager to monitor and control their processes, but doesn't provide much guidance on how to do so. Well, Six Sigma focuses on data, analysis, diagrams, and charts that convey the information needed to make good decisions.

Managing the Quadruple Constraints of Project Management with the Trifecta

Each project has four general objectives, which are also the four constraints of the project:

Scope: Enforce a clear definition of requirements and rigorous change management
Time: better scheduling, immovable deadlines, careful progress monitoring, risk management, and enforces better resource management
Cost: absolute budgets, enforce careful cost controls, and effective forecasting (Proceedings of the Project Management Institute
Quality: enforce unyielding quality targets, careful selection of standards, and realistic assessment of capabilities

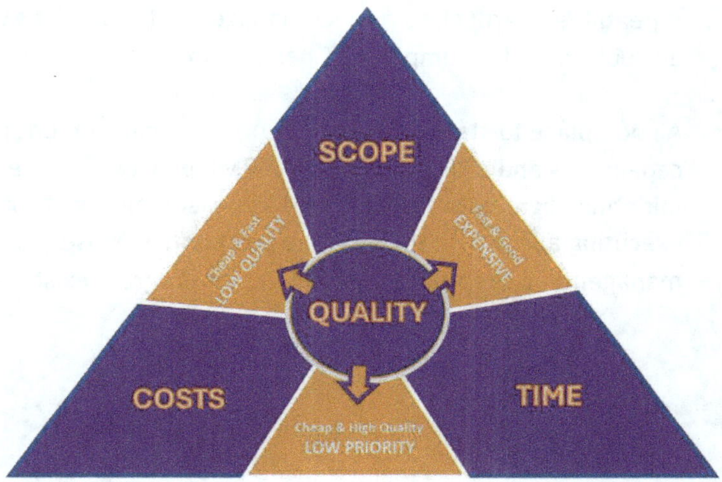

Figure 102. The quadruple constraints of project management

Proceedings of the Project Management Institute Annual Seminars & Symposium. October 3–10, 2002. San Antonio, Texas, USA

Although many professionals hold both a PMP and a Six Sigma Belt, it is not the standard. The project manager should have just enough Six Sigma — maybe a yellow belt — and the Six Sigma Belt should have just enough project management — perhaps a CAPM. Many professionals pursue both certifications to complement their skill sets. PMP provides broad project management knowledge, while Six Sigma offers specialized quality improvement expertise that can be applied across various project types.

On a practical level, a PMP and a Six Sigma Belt should work hand in hand on projects within a PMO. In the meantime, you will play both roles. You will be the project manager and the Six Sigma professional wrapped into one. A review of what's happening in the field shows that very few organizations survive on waterfall (predictive) projects alone. The speed of technological advancements and business processes, and of course, the hybrid nature of the workforce, does not allow that to be sustainable across many industries. Many PMOs are looking for a sustained, repeatable approach to project management that aligns with a PMO Framework, training, and the evaluation of their employees' performance.

A good place to start is to see how project management phases and artifacts align with Six Sigma capabilities and tools. Lining up the PMP phases with the Six Sigma phases is pretty straightforward: Initiating aligns with the define phase, planning aligns with the measure and analyze phases, executing aligns with the improve and control phases, and closing the work. Only in project management does a process, project, or program exist; it can always be improved.

Le 18. PMP/DMAIC Comparison

Project Management Professional: PMBOK		Six Sigma Professional: DMAIC	
Artifact	**Phase**	**Phase**	**Artifact**
Project Charter	Initiation	Define	Project Charter
Roadmap	Planning	Define	Roadmap
Stakeholder Register, RACI Matrix	Planning	Define	Stakeholder Analysis, Team Charter
Project Baselines	Planning	Measure	Budget Baseline, Performance Mgmt. Baseline
Statement of Work	Initiation	Define	Project Vision Statement
Business Case	Initiation	Define	Process Mapping, Project Selection Tool, threats, and opportunity matrix
Requirements	Planning	Define	VOC Requirements Translation and Kano Analysis Value-Stream Mapping, Process Walk Interview Sheet
Network Chart (CPA, PERT)	Planning	Measure	Critical Path Method (CPM)
Flow Charts	Planning	Measure	Flow Charts
Process Maps	Planning	Define	Swimlane Process Maps
Quality Plan	Monitor & Control	Improve	Quality Plan, quality report
Test Plan	Planning	Define	Test plan, New procedure audit
RACI Chart, RAM, LRC Stakeholder Analysis	Initiation	Define	RACI Chart
RAID Log, Risk Analysis	Executing	Improve	Failure Modes and Effects Analysis (FMEA), Five Whys, Regression Analysis, Risk Report
Communication Plan	Planning	Define	Communications Plan
RAG / Traffic Light Status	Monitor & Control	Control	Regulation Diagram
Status Report	Executing		Status Report

Forecasting Reports	Control	Analyze	Control chart
Dashboard	Control	Analyze	Dashboard
Decision Matrix	Executing	Improve	Pareto Chart
Performance Reports	Monitor & Control	Improve	Control chart, Bartlett's Test
Exception Report	Monitor &Control	Control	Regulation Diagram
Agreements	Planning	Define	Agreements

Finding opportunities to bring all three together is an opportunity for the project manager to pull the best of the three to the table as the project progresses. When creating your project charter, review traditional, agile, and Six Sigma project charters to ensure your charter includes all the information needed to move forward. Creating a roadmap for the project is the same for all three approaches in the trifecta.

Where you will see a real difference is when you use Six Sigma to squeeze out time and energy waste in projects. Also, during the iterations, projects will move through design, development, and review. It is at this time that Six Sigma shines. Giving the clients and the sponsors fundamental ways to improve their approaches, requirements, and results is a real game-changer.

Index

www.ingramcontent.com/pod-product-compliance
Lightning Source LLC
LaVergne TN
LVHW080049210926
848481LV00011B/3310